BBC

HOSEA JOEL, AMOS OBADIAH, and JONAH

James E. Sargent

ABINGDON PRESS
Nashville

Hosea through Jonah

Copyright © 1988 by Graded Press

This book is printed on recycled, acid-free paper.

Library of Congress Cataloging-in-Publication Data

Cokesbury basic Bible commentary.
    Basic Bible commentary / by Linda B. Hinton . . . [et al.].
       p.   cm.
    Originally published: Cokesbury basic Bible commentary. Nashville: Graded Press, © 1988.
    ISBN 0-687-02620-2 (pbk. : v. 1 : alk. paper)
    1. Bible—Commentaries. I. Hinton, Linda B. II. Title.
[BS491.2.C65   1994]
220.7—dc20

94-10965
CIP

ISBN 0-687-02634-2 (v. 15, Hosea–Jonah)
ISBN 0-687-02620-2 (v. 1, Genesis)
ISBN 0-687-02621-0 (v. 2, Exodus–Leviticus)
ISBN 0-687-02622-9 (v. 3, Numbers–Deuteronomy)
ISBN 0-687-02623-7 (v. 4, Joshua–Ruth)
ISBN 0-687-02624-5 (v. 5, 1–2 Samuel)
ISBN 0-687-02625-3 (v. 6, 1–2 Kings)
ISBN 0-687-02626-1 (v. 7, 1–2 Chronicles)
ISBN 0-687-02627-X (v. 8, Ezra–Esther)
ISBN 0-687-02628-8 (v. 9, Job)
ISBN 0-687-02629-6 (v. 10, Psalms)
ISBN 0-687-02630-X (v. 11, Proverbs–Song of Solomon)
ISBN 0-687-02631-8 (v. 12, Isaiah)
ISBN 0-687-02632-6 (v. 13, Jeremiah–Lamentations)
ISBN 0-687-02633-4 (v. 14, Ezekiel–Daniel)
ISBN 0-687-02635-0 (v. 16, Micah–Malachi)
ISBN 0-687-02636-9 (v. 17, Matthew)
ISBN 0-687-02637-7 (v. 18, Mark)
ISBN 0-687-02638-5 (v. 19, Luke)
ISBN 0-687-02639-3 (v. 20, John)
ISBN 0-687-02640-7 (v. 21, Acts)
ISBN 0-687-02642-3 (v. 22, Romans)
ISBN 0-687-02643-1 (v. 23, 1–2 Corinthians)
ISBN 0-687-02644-X (v. 24, Galatians–Ephesians)
ISBN 0-687-02645-8 (v. 25, Philippians–2 Thessalonians)
ISBN 0-687-02646-6 (v. 26, 1 Timothy–Philemon)
ISBN 0-687-02647-4 (v. 27, Hebrews)
ISBN 0-687-02648-2 (v. 28, James–Jude)
ISBN 0-687-02649-0 (v. 29, Revelation)
ISBN 0-687-02650-4 (complete set of 29 vols.)

99 00 01 02 03—10 9 8 7 6 5 4 3

MANUFACTURED IN THE UNITED STATES OF AMERICA

Contents

Outline of Hosea through Jonah

Hosea

I. The Prophet and His Message (1:1–3:5)
  A. Superscription/Title (1:1)
  B. Gomer and the children (1:2-9)
  C. Restoration promised (1:10–2:1)
  D. Unfaithfulness and punishment (2:2-13)
  E. Restoration and redemption (2:14-23)
  F. The restoration of Gomer (3:1-5)
II. Judgment on Israel (4:1–5:15)
  A. The Lord's controversy with Israel (4:1-19)
  B. The treachery of Ephraim (5:1-15)
III. Catastrophe for Israel (6:1–8:14)
  A. Shallow repentance and intrigue (6:1–7:7)
  B. Israel loses its identity (7:8-16)
  C. Israel's death sentence (8:1-14)
IV. Idolatry and the Love of God (9:1–11:12)
  A. Ephraim's idolatry and punishment (9:1-17)
  B. Israel's king; Bethel's idol (10:1-15)
  C. The love of God (11:1-11)
V. Oracles of Israel's Doom (11:12–14:9)
  A. Israel's evil and doom (11:12–12:14)
  B. Toward an inexorable end (13:1-13)
  C. A severe grace (14:1-8)
  D. Instructions to the reader (14:9)

Joel

I. Introduction to Joel's Prophecy (1:1–2:11)
   A. Title (1:1)
   B. A call for national lament (1:2-14)
   C. A terrible crises (1:15-20)
   D. The day of the Lord (2:1-11)
II. Oracles Concerning the Future (2:12–3:21)
   A. Call for national repentance (2:12-17)
   B. The promise of fertility (2:18-27)
   C. The outpouring of the Spirit (2:28-32)
   D. God's judgment of oppressors (3:1-21)

Amos

I. Oracles Against Foreign Nations (1:1–2:16)
   A. Title (1:1-2)
   B. Oracles against the nations (1:3–2:16)
II. Oracles Concerning Israel (3:1–4:13)
   A. Peril and privilege of election (3:1-15)
   B. Oracles against Israel's excesses (4:1-13)
III. Israel's Inevitable Doom (5:1–6:14)
   A. Israel's just reward for sin (5:1-27)
   B. Oracles of an inevitable doom (6:1-14)
IV. Visions and Confrontation (7:1-17)
   A. Judgment and visions (7:1-9)
   B. Conflict and confrontation (7:10-17)
V. Visions of Israel's Doom (8:1–9:15)
   A. A vision and an indictment (8:1-14)
   B. The finality of Israel's doom (9:1-15)
   C. A promise of restoration (9:11-15)

Obadiah

I. Title and Introduction (verse 1)
II. Destruction of Edom (verses 2-14)
    A. A warning (verses 2-4)
    B. Complete destruction (verses 5-9)
    C. Reason for judgment (verses 10-14)
III. The Day of the Lord (verses 15-21)
    A. The day of the Lord (verses 15-16)
    B. A role for survivors (verse 17)
    C. Promise of Israel's restoration (verses 18-21)

Jonah

I. The Great Refusal (1:1-3)
II. Jonah Punished (1:4-16)
III. Jonah's Rescue (1:17–2:10)
IV. The Great Mission (3:1–4:11)
    A. Jonah's obedience (3:1-4)
    B. Nineveh's repentance (3:5-9)
    C. Jonah's rebuke (3:10–4:11)

Introduction

In this commentary we will examine some of the most extraordinary writings and individuals found in the entire Bible. We know them as *prophets*. During the long and often troubled history of Israel, uniquely gifted individuals emerged as spokesmen for God. These messengers were of various backgrounds and from different parts of the nation. However, each of them was vitally concerned about and aware of the immediate events of history. What made them unique was their keen sense of the inexorable ethical and spiritual demand of God on the people of God in the midst of that history.

Throughout Israel's history four forces were always in tension with the people of God as they attempted to live out their lives of faith: syncretism, military alliances and alignments, economic disparity and oppression, and historical forces impinging on Israel's faith.

Syncretism

As far back as the beginning of the conquest of the promised territory, the Israelite conquerors had been tempted to adopt some of the religious behaviors of the native population. This assimilation is called *syncretism*. The fertility rites of Baalism that took their cue from the fertility and produce of the land had a very powerful appeal. The threat of syncretism was one of the reasons prophets emerged.

Military Alliances

As the nation became more involved in the ways of the surrounding world and thus more mature in the ways of the world, it began to trust more and more in its military and international military alignments and alliances. Along with a developing maturity came a moving away from what had characterized earlier history when Israelites had no option but the utter dependence upon God that had characterized the years of trial and testing during and after the Exodus. The prophets interpreted the growing independence from God as apostasy or faithlessness.

Economic Concerns

Over the course of time Israel changed from what had been primarily a nomadic existence to a more sophisticated society and economy with many large urban centers. However, along with the development of cities (Isaiah 9:10; Hosea 8:14; Micah 3:10) came remarkable economic growth. As wealth became more possible and widespread, the distinction between the 'haves' and the 'have-nots' increased. Along with this growth came social distinctions and unjust as well as unfair practices perpetrated by the wealthy against the poor and disenfranchised. Today the modern reader understands these excesses and injustices to be wrong. But it took the courageous and sensitive prophetic insight to identify the wrongs as sin in God's sight. Among the prophets, Amos and Micah were especially keen to identify the excesses of wealth and power as oppressive social injustices.

Historical Forces

Finally, Israel lived out her life amidst other nations in the world of international history. The most dominant nation during the time of the prophets' history was the proud and terrible Assyrian empire. The military and political concerns stirred by this menacing empire punctuate nearly all of the prophets' works.

Assyria's advances were sporadic, not consistently

powerful. However, for the first time in her history Israel had to contend with powers that exceeded her capacity to fight effectively. In the formative years of wandering and conquering of the Promised Land, the national understanding of God centered on a tribal deity concerned with the protection of the favored people of God's choosing. However, when historical forces became much larger and engulfed Israel in the tides of international power politics and military maneuvering, the small God-thinking could not long endure. Therefore, the prophets served a special function by enlarging the peoples' theological understanding of history. The people of Israel had to develop a much larger conception of who their God was. Assyria's might and conquests shattered the notion of limited and local tribal gods. Israel's history was a part of a much larger phenomenon. Amos stresses this larger notion in summarizing the freedom and sovereignty of God. As Assyria shattered Israel's smaller conceptions, the prophets envisioned a much larger God with international moral demands and expectations. Israel's God would now be God who could work with the Assyrians as well as with Israel.

Compounding the catastrophes of Assyrian incursions and military superiority, the once-proud united empire of Israel established by King David had suffered a terrible civil war. Upon the death of Solomon the ten tribes in the north revolted against Solomon's son and formed the nation Israel. Two tribes remained loyal to the Davidic throne. These two tribes formed the small nation of Judah. For the balance of their existence these two nations engaged in constant civil war. One of history's ironies is that just at the moment when the nation of Israel needed to maintain its unity, it split into rival states. The tragedy of Israel's enslavement and deportation fills the eighth century. Judah's demise would follow at the end of the seventh century.

The Book of the Twelve or the Minor Prophets

This commentary will concentrate on the first five of the twelve prophets, or the minor prophets. For centuries the Book of the Twelve has suffered from the name the *Minor Prophets*. The implication is, of course, that these works are in some sense less important or of less significance in the entire biblical revelation than the longer and better-known gigantic figures of Isaiah, Jeremiah, and Ezekiel. In fact, the major prophets are of such length that each of them fills an entire scroll by itself. The Twelve, on the other hand, are not long enough to warrant a single scroll for each. Therefore, the books were written together on one scroll. The scroll containing the entire corpus of the shorter prophets is therefore best referred to as The Twelve. The reason they are called the minor prophets has only to do with their relative brevity in comparison to the major works of Isaiah, Jeremiah, and Ezekiel.

The order of the books, their *canonical* order, follows what the original compilers understood to be the correct chronological order from the eighth to the fourth centuries B.C. However, these ancient rabbis did not have the advantage of modern critical scholarship and multiple sources for their examination. A good deal of modern scholarship has been addressed to the identification of specific historical eras in which these writings first emerged.

The five prophets with which this commentary is concerned are Hosea, Joel, Amos, Obadiah, and Jonah. These prophets are individuals called by God who have a unique awareness of activity through events and history as well as the moral demands of God. Each of these prophets strives with all his might to make the moral demand and theological implications clear in relation to the very real, threatening, stimulating, and frightening swirl of real historical, social, and economic events.

Introduction to Hosea

Hosea is the first of the Twelve. His name occurs in the title and in the heading. The name *Hosea* does appear in other places in the Hebrew Scriptures (see 2 Kings 15:30; 1 Chronicles 27:20). He is identified as the son of Beeri. We know very little about him except that he was probably fairly young when he began his ministry, as he was of marriageable age. His career spanned nearly a quarter of a century of Israel's most difficult history.

Hosea's work began during the peaceful years of Jeroboam II (786–746 B.C.). His work concludes sometime around the time of the horrendous defeat of Israel by the Assyrians in 721 B.C.

Ironically, even Israel's peaceful years were disrupted both by internal and external developments. Internally Jeroboam's own son Zechariah (746–737) succeeded to the throne. Within six months Shallum ben Jabesh gained the throne by assassinating Zechariah. The internal politics of Israel quickly became marred by conspiracy and murder. Jabesh was himself assassinated within a month by Menahem (745–738) (see 2 Kings 15:8-16). Given the fact of Assyrian expansion and the grave threat that expansion posed for Israel, Menahem expediently decided to become a vassal state to the Assyrian ruler Tiglath-pileser III. Israel had to pay an enormous tax as tribute to the Assyrians (see 2 Kings 15:19). The palace intrigue continued with the rapid accession of Pekahiah (738–737). Pekah ben Ramaliah (737–732) then seized the throne. He very soon attempted to form an alliance against the detested Assyrians. Israel attempted to force her southern sister nation, Judah, into the alliance by means of a war. The Syro-Ephraimitic war forms a part of the backdrop against which Hosea must be read.

The Assyrian ruler Tiglath-pileser attacked the rebellious nations. Israel's king, Hosea ben Elah (732–724) surrendered. Later on he attempted to secure aid from Egypt (see Hosea 9:3; 11:5). Under the onslaught of Assyria, Damascus/Syria collapsed in 732; Israel in 721/722; Egypt in 663, and finally Judah in 587.

In Assyria, Shalmaneser (727–722) succeeded Tiglath-pileser. Hoshea, the king of Israel, foolishly withheld the payment required from vassal states. Angered by the foolhardy challenge, the Assyrians made Hoshea Shalmaneser's captive (Hosea 13:10). The capital city was besieged; Israel's armies were soundly defeated. Hosea sees the collapse of all Samaria/Israel (Hosea 13:16).

Hosea used various metaphors to describe the relationship which existed between God and Israel as the people of God. The most frequently used metaphor is that of the unfaithful wife as harlot. Harlotry characterized the people of God. Hosea spoke to his own people. Throughout his work he showed familiarity with major centers of Israel's land: Samaria (7:1; 8:5; 10:5, 7), Bethel (4:15; 5:8; 10:5; 12:4), and Gilgal (4:15; 9:15; 12:11).

The book can be easily divided into two major sections. The first part centers on the prophet's experience with marriage and family (chapters 1–4). The second part consists of loosely joined material that defies simple attempts to organize or outline (chapters 5–14).

Hosea 1–3

Introduction to These Chapters

The first three chapters in the book of Hosea introduce us to the prophet and his message. These chapters include an introductory superscription, followed by material related to Hosea's marriage and his spiritual disciplines.

These three chapters may be outlined as follows.
   I. Superscription/Title (1:1)
  II. Gomer and the Children (1:2-9)
 III. Restoration Promised (1:10–2:1)
  IV. Unfaithfulness and Punishment (2:2-13)
   V. Restoration and Redemption (2:14-23)
  VI. The Restoration of Gomer (3:1-5)

Superscription / Title (1:1)

As with other Hebrew prophets, the word of the Lord comes directly to the prophet (see Jeremiah 1:1-5; Ezekiel 1:3; Joel 1:1; Jonah 1:1; Micah 1:1; Zephaniah 1:1). The prophet's work is not of his own authority. The prophet's authority is from the inspiration and leading of God. During the ministry of Hosea and others, there were others who claimed to be prophets as well. Their utterances are lost. We learn of them only as we read and hear the objections and observations of the biblical prophets, the true prophets. People of the day had to decide which prophets to heed. Both true and false prophets made the claim of legitimacy and authority. As a rule the true prophet of God did not speak of easier alternatives or the easier way out of the moral and political quandaries confronting Israel and Judah. The true spokesman for God spoke of the harsh realities of judgment and of a severe salvation for the people.

The name *Hosea* means *salvation* or *deliverance.*

The list of kings begins with Judean kings, thus suggesting a Judean editor: Uzziah 783-742; Jotham 740-731; Ahaz 731-715; Hezekiah 715-686. Israel's king Jeroboam ben Joash (786-746) is the only one mentioned, but Hosea's prophecy continued after Jeroboam's death.

Gomer and the Children (1:2-9)

One of the most difficult issues in interpreting Hosea is his marriage to the harlot Gomer. Did Hosea know that Gomer was a harlot when he first married her? Is the entire heart-rending episode an allegory that means something else altogether? Symbolic acts by prophets are not uncommon (see Isaiah 8:1-4; Jeremiah 27). We will be closer to the heart of the matter if we can imagine Hosea writing at a later time, subsequent to his marriage. He discovered first by intuition, perhaps, that his wife, once the apple of his eye, had strayed. How else can we understand the heartbroken prophet's insight into the pathos of the God of Israel? But Hosea is able to appropriate theological insights from his own bitter experience. He learns of the relationship between God and Israel from the earliest years of first love, the Exodus and the wilderness. He learns of the profound love of God for the people, a love that could not let them go.

Note that Hosea gives no narrative of his call into the prophetic ministry (in contrast to Isaiah 1:1; Jeremiah 1:1-4; Ezekiel 1–2).

Hosea's marriage is a dramatic act of obedience. Through this action Hosea shows the indictment of Israel for her sin. *Adultery* (NIV; NRSV = *whoredom*) means sexual promiscuity (see 2:5; 3:3; 4:12-14; 9:1). Israel had succumbed to the temptation to adopt some of the Canaanite fertility religion attitudes and behaviors. For Hosea, the metaphor of harlotry is the same as the despicable reality of Israel's apostasy.

Gomer is the daughter of Diblaim. The name *Diblaim* may be a variation on the place Diblathaim (see Numbers 33:46; Jeremiah 48:22). The name may also be derived from the word that means *fig cakes*, thus suggesting that she was a woman who could be had for the price of two cakes.

In verse 4, God commands Hosea to name the first boy *Jezreel*. In Hebrew the name can be interpreted two ways. First it can mean *he sows*, which implies fertility and blessing. The second possibility is a reference to the Valley of Jezreel, a scene of terrible bloodshed (see Judges 6–7; also 2 Kings 9:17-26; 10:1-11), which would imply woe. The second child, a daughter, is named *Lo-ruhamah* (which means *not pitied*). Israel will be left without compassion.

Verse 7 is probably an addition by a Judean editor. God will save Judah by other means, not warfare.

Hosea suspects that his second child is not his. The third child confirms his worst suspicions as he names the child *Lo-ammi (Not my people)*. Hosea alludes to the language of the covenant in which God had promised that Israel would be the chosen people (see Exodus 6:7; 19:5-6; Isaiah 40:1; Jeremiah 31:31-33). The name now suggests that the covenant is either no longer in force at worst, or in great peril at best.

Restoration Promised (1:10–2:1)

In this oracle God makes the promise of a great hope for the future. Since this oracle is unique, nothing else like it exists in Hosea's prophecy, some scholars question its authenticity as Hosea's work. It follows closely on the awful symbolism of God's rejection of Israel. It could have been first uttered after the military disasters of 733, during a time in which people asked about the meaning of the current history.

The promises to the ancient patriarchs will survive the judgment of the present crisis.

Only here are the people of Israel called *the sons* (NIV; NRSV = *children) of the living God.*

The day of Jezreel (verse 11) is the same as *the day of Midian* in Isaiah 9:4 (see also Judges 7:15-25).

Unfaithfulness and Punishment (2:2-13)

The scene is now one of a court proceeding with the husband as the plaintiff. What is the purpose of the proceedings? Does Hosea want to suggest guilt and subsequent punishment? The purpose of the process is reconciliation. The descriptions indicate a time of prosperity (verses 5, 8) and utter confidence in the Canaanite religious cult (verses 11, 13).

The *lovers* (verse 13) are the baals of the land. These were local gods believed to be responsible for fertility in the land. Israel had become enamored with this religious system.

The appeal in verse 2 is followed by a strong warning (verses 3-4).

The baals (verse 5) are considered by many to be the source of fertility and blessings of the basic necessities of life: food, clothing material, and the commodities of an abundant life. The mother's behavior is a deliberate and willful act in defiance of God.

Verses 6-8 contain the first of three introductory *Therefore* statements. The first is that the rituals of Baalism will bring no results, no matter how desperate and expressive the people become. But will they become as energetic in attempting to reconcile with God? *Silver and gold* indicate a time of opulence and prosperity that Israel wasted on foolish worship.

The second announcement, in verses 9-18, asserts that

God will destroy the relationship between Israel and Baalism. Natural disaster will take away the blessings of grain, wine, wool, and flax (see above in verses 5, 8).

Verse 11 mentions *feasts*. Three major feasts were central in Israel's religious life (see Exodus 23:14-17; 34:18-23). The *new moon* celebrated the beginning of the month. The *sabbath* was the weekly rest from labor.

According to verse 12, God will bring about natural disaster, thus robbing Israel of her needs.

Restoration and Redemption (2:14-23)

The cult of Baal (verse 13) is Israel's harlotry. Here is the third announcement: God will once again restore the relationship with Israel. Israel will see that it is God and not Baal that gives the blessings from the earth.

The narrative of the events of the *Valley of Achor* occurs in the book of Joshua (7:1-26; see also Isaiah 65:10). During the campaign against Jericho, one man violated the oath of destruction by taking for himself and his family gold and silver from the destroyed city. Because of his sin, the Israelites failed in the first battle for Ai. The early Israelites believed very strongly that the entire society suffered when one of its members sinned. The man, Achan, was discovered. He and his entire family were summarily executed by stoning. The name of the place was called the *Valley of Achor*, which means the *Valley of Trouble*. Hosea takes this dreadful memory of defeat and shame and uses it to show how God will use even the worst circumstances for good purposes.

In verse 16, the prophet speaks using both an eschatalogical and oracle form. The *day of the* LORD (see Amos 5:18-20) is an historical and theological concept. Israel believed that history moves towards a time when God will have the last say, the last act. In that day, then, God will finally judge between nations, evils will be judged, and accountings will be made for actions. The popular conception, of course, was that Israel would find herself beside God, justifiably proud of her standing and relishing the final discipline and punishment of her age-old oppressors.

The words for *husband* and *baal* in Hebrew are very similar. Here Hosea plays on the word to show how Israel will no longer call the local god *husband* or *master*. Nor will Israel continue being a harlot or mistress. The marriage relationship will be reestablished. All evidences of Baal worship will cease.

According to verse 18, the entire creation will be affected by the renewed relationship. The covenant will be renewed with animals (note the role of the animals is reversed from verse 12). The threat of war will be removed from Israel.

In verse 19, God speaks as a man would speak to a woman preparing for marriage. Betrothal is the final step before actually living together. This will be an unconditional covenant. Five central concepts form the bride's price: *righteousness, justice, steadfast love, mercy* or *compassion,* and *faithfulness.*

These five theological concepts form the foundation of Hosea's thinking. None of them corresponds exactly with modern, Western ways of thinking. Each of them has rootage deep within the traditions of Israel and especially in the nature and character of God. Modern readers must be very careful not to make of these rich and vibrant concepts a rigid legalism. Righteousness means the fulfillment of the demands of a relationship in any context. Many kinds of relationships impinge upon individuals at any given time: spouse with spouse, neighbor with neighbor, native with sojourner, rich with the poor, individual with God. Each of these relationships carries with it certain expectations. Performing the appropriate responsibilities in the relationship maintains the relationship. Thus, maintaining social order and relationships depends upon righteousness. Violating the righteous means ripping the

HOSEA THROUGH JONAH

social fabric. Sin never occurs in isolation; it always has an impact on the balance of society.

Justice is closely related to righteousness. Justice is the vertical weave to righteousness (the horizontal weave) in the fabric of society. Justice has to do with the way things ought to be in God's sight.

Relationships are characterized by steadfast love or loyal love. As God has steadfastly refused to give up on Israel, so the people of Israel must maintain steadfast love toward each other and toward God.

Characteristic of God as well is compassion or mercy. The Hebrew word for mercy comes from the same root word meaning *womb*. Therefore, mercy takes on the characteristics of God's relationship with Israel through the deliverance from slavery, rescue from certain death at the sea, forgiveness, and fulfillment of promises.

The final element of Hosea's theological understanding is faithfulness. The history of Israel shows God stubbornly remaining faithful to God's promises even though Israel at nearly every turn gives sufficient reason for God to despair and concede to the whims of a fickle people.

For Hosea to *know* God means an understanding of all five notions. Here God takes on the responsibility of maintaining the relationship's integrity.

Verses 21-22 explain that, after God has established the relationship, other events in nature are set into motion.

I will sow ([NRSV; NIV = *plant*] verse 23) is an allusion to the name *Jezreel*.

The Restoration of Gomer (3:1-5)

This chapter begins with instructions similar to those found in 1:2-9. Here the narrative is in the first person. Three parts make up the chapter: a divine command, the doing of the directive, and an interpretation of the action. For other prophetic acts see 2 Kings 13:15-19; Jeremiah

13:1-11; Ezekiel 12:1-11. Though the woman is not named, it is assumed that she is Gomer.

In this short narrative Hosea sets out the basic drama. God returns to seek an individual. The example of God's love is set by God and not by human beings. God is still God. Even though the people of Israel have been unfaithful, God will woo them back. Only God's stubborn refusal to accept no for an answer makes a future possible.

The LORD said to me (verse 1) is reminiscent of Isaiah 8:1; Jeremiah 3:6; Amos 7:8, 15; 8:2. *Raisin cakes* are delicacies used in pagan festivities (see 2 Samuel 6:19; Isaiah 16:7; Jeremiah 7:18).

A *shekel* equals approximately eleven grams; a *homer* is six and one-half bushels; and a *lethech* equals approximately three bushels. The image Hosea creates is that redemption is very costly.

According to verses 3-4, Israel's future behavior will include a new royal institution and the elimination of the public cult.

Ephods were used in learning the divine will. *Teraphim* (NRSV; NIV = *idol*) is the name for images, sometimes used in household shrines.

Afterward (verse 5) implies that there will be a future—more history in which the people of God will be faithful. The people will return to their God and seek God as they had during the days of the Exodus. The reference to David as king is probably an addition by a Judean editor, since in all previous utterances Hosea has stressed images from the Exodus and wilderness experience.

§ § § § § § §

The Message of Hosea 1–3

The first three chapters of Hosea are a remarkable narrative of the stubborn and long-suffering love of God. What are some of the truths we learn from these chapters?

§ Nothing can stop God's love.
§ When God gives an instruction, a man or a woman must obey.
§ Marriage is a sacred institution.
§ We can learn of God's feelings by praying.
§ God is not far removed from our lives; God is close and feels the pain of faithlessness and sin.
§ God refuses to be divorced from the realities of human life.
§ The reality of God allows us to interpret the events of our lives.
§ God can use even the worst circumstances for good.
§ God sets the example for all people to follow.

§ § § § § § §

Hosea 4–5

Introduction to These Chapters

Chapter 4 begins the second major part of Hosea's work. With but two exceptions (chapter 11 in which Hosea presents the wonderful image of the tender and loving father, and 14:3-9 in which Hosea presents a bright vision of the future) the balance of the book presents little more than a people and a nation in catastrophe and collapse. Chapter 4 does have some unity to it, with a thoroughgoing indictment of priests, the cult, and idols. Judgment is the characteristic tone and intent of chapters 4 and 5. Here is an outline of these chapters.

I. The Lord's Controversy with Israel (4:1-19)
   A. God's controversy (4:1-3)
   B. The case against the priests (4:4-10)
   C. The case against the cult (4:11-14)
   D. Ephraim is joined to idols (4:15-19)
II. The Treachery of Ephraim (5:1-15)
   A. A despicable treachery (5:1-7)
   B. War between brothers (5:8-14)
   C. The threat of an absent God (5:15)

The Lord's Controversy with Israel (4:1-19)

Woven into Israel's tradition is the strand of covenant. Throughout the ancient world, covenants were a common practice between stronger and weaker nations. The covenant contained several standard elements:

(1) A preamble comes first, in which the king or ruler who gives the covenant is identified and the reason for his authority is listed. Covenants were always from the stronger party to the weaker.

(2) The history giving birth to the covenant is then reviewed. In Israel's tradition the best example is the rehearsal of God's saving action in the Exodus (see Exodus 20), *I am the LORD your God, who brought you out of the land of Egypt. . . .*

(3) Stipulations are then listed. The vassal/weaker state is to obey these rules. In the Hebrew tradition the stipulations are called the Decalogue, or what are commonly called the Ten Commandments.

(4) Generally the covenant is stored and read publicly.

(5) Witnesses would then be listed.

(6) Finally, blessings and curses are listed. If the vassal/weaker nation obeys the covenant then blessings will follow. However, violation of the covenant will invoke the curses inflicted or exacted by the offended sovereign state.

Hosea draws on this tradition of covenant relationship. Israel has violated the covenant and may expect to be cursed by God.

God's Controversy (4:1-3)

In verses 1-3, Hosea uses the word *rib* (NIV – *charge*; NRSV = *indictment*) to describe God's controversy with Israel. The word *rib* is taken from court of law proceedings. The word means a *complaint*. In a trial proceeding, the plaintiff would bring the complaint to the judges. Here the word is used initially in a negative way. Then it is used with respect to specific actions. In this instance, God will act the role both of prosecutor and judge. The prophet acts as a herald who will announce the findings of God. The people would have no difficulty understanding the court of law metaphor.

The land is very, very important to the people of

Israel. Far more than merely a place or resource, the land is the gift of God; it belongs to God (see 9:3). The land is one of the means by which God blesses the people (see 2:8-9). Recall that in 1:2 the land serves as a part of the covenant relationship between God and the people. Any reference to land, therefore, becomes a reference to either great blessing or horrendous curse.

The first sins listed are those of omission: no faithfulness, no devotion or kindness/steadfast love, no knowledge of God. Faithfulness, steadfast love, and knowledge of God are central elements in Hosea's work (see 2:19-20; 4:6; 5:4, 7; 6:3, 6; 10:12; 11:3-4; 12:6). To know God means much more than simple affirmation of belief. To know God is to acknowledge God's claim on life and ethics and to do the will of God. God does not delight in sacrifice (see 6:6).

Specific sins are then listed (in verse 2) which violate the Ten Commandments (Exodus 20:2-17): swearing (see Exodus 20:7), lying in both legal matters and later on in commercial trade (see Exodus 20:16; 23:1, 7; Deuteronomy 25:13-16), murder (Exodus 20:13), stealing (see Exodus 20:15; 21:16), and adultery (see Exodus 20:14; Leviticus 20:10). In biblical religion there is a very strong relationship between social morality and religious belief. The two are intertwined and cannot be understood apart from each other.

According to verse 3, when the covenant is violated the entire creation suffers (see Genesis 8:21; Romans 8:20).

The Case Against the Priests (4:4-10)

This indictment begins with a restatement of the *rib*, the controversy. The tone sounds like a rebuttal to an argument posed by some of the hearers. With some imagination perhaps we can hear the argument posed by listeners who did not want to hear what the prophet said. Hosea uses this implied dialogue frequently. Amos had to resist the arguments of others as well (see Amos 7:10-17).

The priests against whom Hosea speaks are the official priests who earn their livelihood doing the official work of the religious life of the nation. The term used by scholars for the official national religion with its attendant functions and duties is *cult*. This term should not be confused with the twentieth-century notion of cult as a different and often strange religious group. The priests against whom Hosea speaks are cultic priests. By the same token, the prophets against whom the biblical prophets speak are cultic priests.

Here Hosea criticizes the priests for giving up the legitimate work of true religion for the activities of the cult.

Destroy your mother (verse 5) refers to the destruction of family members (see the similar references in Jeremiah 22:26; Amos 7:17).

Knowledge means more than mere academic learning. Knowledge means both learning and obeying. The *law of your God* refers to the Torah, the law. However, law means much more than merely a set of rules. In Hebrew tradition law means the revelation of God's truth.

As Israel grew, the nation moved further away from the covenant expectations (see verses 7-10). The priesthood had become just another way to make a good living, rather than the high calling to teach the revelation of God. The priests had given in completely to a religion of pure ritual. They had forgotten that their work was essentially a moral and intellectual work. The prophet also implies that the moral level of the people cannot go higher than the moral level of their priests. Indeed, the people will become like their priests.

God's punishment of the priests and people alike is put in the form of futility curses (for examples see Deuteronomy 28:30, 38-40). Hosea uses the term *prostitution* (NIV; NRSV = *whoredom*) to encompass the phenomenon of syncretism, and syncretism is apostasy or faithlessness. All of the habits and rituals of Baalism will prove utterly useless.

The Case Against the Cult (4:11-14)

The prophet continues with a scathing indictment of the cult. Verse 11 sounds like a proverb, or an observation drawn from common life.

The *piece of wood* (NRSV; NIV = *wooden idol*) may well have been an image, or an idol (see Isaiah 44:13-15; Jeremiah 10:3), or perhaps an Asherah (see Deuteronomy 16:21; Judges 6:25-26).

Very frequently the shrines or worship centers of the Baal cult were on hilltops or in a stand of trees. *Daughters play the whore* (NRSV; NIV = *daughters when they turn to prostitution*) may refer to the custom of virgins giving up their virginity as a part of their marriage preparation in the shrine.

According to verse 14, however, the problem is not solely with the women. The men are part of the problem as well. Both men and women include sexual experiences as a part of the cultic worship they practice. This kind of behavior is far removed from the behavior God expects from the people of the covenant. The oracle concludes with another observation about life. A spirit of harlotry leads to a lack of understanding, and the lack of understanding will inevitably lead to the individual's and the nation's ruin.

Ephraim Is Joined to Idols (4:15-19)

The prophet's words should be sufficient warning to the nation to the south, Judah (see other references to Judah in 5:5, 10, 13; 6:4).

Gilgal is a sanctuary in the Jordan valley north of Jericho (see Joshua 4:19-20; 5:9-10; Hosea 9:15; 12:11).

Beth-aven is a nickname with bad connotations for Bethel (see 5:8; 10:5; Amos 5:5).

Hosea uses *Ephraim* as another name for Israel.

Worship had become little more than an excuse for wild sexual orgies. In Hebrew the word for *wind* (NRSV; NIV = *whirlwind*) is the same word as *spirit* (*ruach*). The prophet therefore implies that the spirit of the people had ensnared them and would lead to their ruin.

A Despicable Treachery (5:1-7)

The leaders and priests (recall the priests in 4:4-10) of the nation have misled the people. In this short oracle the leaders are summoned to hear God's judgment. God will punish them all. Hosea's understanding of judgment includes inevitable punishment as a part of redemption. The sins of both leaders and people cannot be overlooked or quickly passed by.

Mizpah and *Tabor* are both cultic shrine centers. The location of Mizpah could be one of two places: in Gilead, in the Transjordan (see Judges 10:17), or north of Jerusalem in the territory of Benjamin (see Judges 20:1-3; 21:1-8). Tabor is a mountain in the eastern part of the Valley of Jezreel (see Judges 4:6).

Shittim also contained a shrine (see Numbers 25:1).

In verses 3-7 the prophet speaks further on the theme of Israel's apostasy. From the descriptions of cultic worship, scholars suggest that this prophecy occurs early in Hosea's ministry, probably during the reign of Jeroboam II.

Hosea again uses the alternative name *Ephraim* for Israel. The word *defiled* (NRSV; NIV = *corrupt*) alludes to ritual defilement or uncleanness which would remove an individual from the presence of God. The defilement cannot be quickly resolved through cultic practices. Indeed, the actions of people indicate an inability to return to their God.

Central to Hosea's work is the paramount question, Is it possible to believe in repentance and conversion? Throughout his work Hosea wrestles long and hard with the harsh realities of human intransigence and sin. However, he wrestles equally with the power of God. Will God's love be sufficient to the need of Israel now ensnared almost inextricably in her sin? In an earlier prophecy Amos had declared without question that God's law would prevail. Israel had sinned and would surely pay the penalty. But the question Amos left was whether or not God's love was equal to God's law.

The *pride* (NRSV; NIV = *arrogance*) of Israel means the dependence upon cultic worship.

Judah is the kingdom to the south. This section of text may be an addition by a later editor declaring that what happens to Israel can surely happen to Judah as well if that nation does not mend its ways.

According to verse 6, all of the efforts of the people to see God through the worship of the cult will fail. Here *flocks and herds* means sacrifice. Worse than not being able to find God, God will become absent from the people (see 5:15).

The oracle concludes in verse 7 with an accusation of crime, that is, faithlessness, and a prediction of punishment. The evidence of the crime is *illegitimate children* (recall Hosea's earlier episode with his own family, one of whom is named *Not my people*).

War Between Brothers (5:8-14)

The scene shifts without warning from cultic worship to a military-political arena. Civil war continued throughout the tragic centuries following the division upon Solomon's death. Perhaps no greater tragedy occurred than the attempt by the Northern Kingdom, Israel, to secure Judah's support in the confrontation of Assyria. Pekah, king of Israel, had allied himself with Rezin, of the kingdom of Damascus, against the Assyrians led by Tiglath-pileser. King Ahaz of Judah remained unconvinced. The two would-be challengers besieged Jerusalem. The war is called the

Syro-Ephraimitic War (see 2 Kings 15:27-30). Ahaz, the grandson of Uzziah, found himself in the impossible position of defeat by allied forces. Incredibly, he appealed to the Assyrians for their help in breaking the siege by the allies from the north. Not surprisingly, Israel was defeated in 733 and Pekah was assassinated. Hoshea became the king of Israel as vassal to the victorious Assyrians. The victory of Judah, however, was an illusory one. It hastened the demise of the nation since it too became essentially a vassal state.

The entire oracle begins in verse 8 with the sound of the horn summoning men to battle. Gibeah and Ramah are fortified towns (see 1 Kings 15:16-22) along with Bethaven/Bethel, along the line of march taken by the invading Assyrians. All these cities are in the land traditionally associated with Benjamin (see Joshua 18:21).

Hosea obviously places no trust in alliances with any nation against the power of Assyria (see verse 9).

Landmarks established legal boundaries. To remove landmarks is to illegally alter the ownership of land, which is tantamount to encroaching upon others' territory (see Deuteronomy 19:14; Proverbs 22:28). God is not merely mildly interested in proper procedure. The deep emotion of wrath stirs within God's own soul. The prophet is not afraid to speak of God in human emotional terms.

The section concludes in verses 11-12 with a lament. Israel had turned to an historical enemy against the brothers to the south. By the same token the brothers to the south had looked to the powerful empire from the east against the Northern Kingdom. Rot and decay characterize both peoples of God. God is already at work through the history that affects both nations.

According to verses 13-14, even with history at work threatening to engulf both peoples, no one recognizes God at work. They see no moral dimension to their political and military actions.

Sickness and *wound* (NRSV; NIV = *sores*) are allusions to military disasters (see Isaiah 1:5; Jeremiah 30:12). What the nations do not yet realize is that the source of their wound is God! They are dealing with symptoms; God will deal with the disease. The primary force at work in history is God; no other power is as significant or powerful. But the people do not yet realize this. God will stalk the people of the covenant throughout history.

The Threat of an Absent God (5:15)

This verse separates verses 10-14 and 6:1-3. The verse serves to make the transition from the one passage to the other. Though disaster overwhelms both nations, God may still return. Note that the word *return* (NRSV; NIV = *go back*) is used to describe God's action. Earlier Hosea had noted that the people themselves could not return due to their sin. But God can change God's mind; God can return. Hosea could hardly make his point any stronger. God's anger and wrath have at their center not the ultimate purpose of distance from the people. Rather, God seeks reconciliation with the people.

During times of stress people always seek God. But Hosea has already noted repeatedly that the people tended towards the religion of the cult. We can almost see them anxiously carrying out their sacrifices, their prayers, and their orgy-like worship wondering if it would be enough to get God to smile upon them. Here God speaks with firm resolve; the seeking must be wholehearted (see Amos 5:4). Little more could be as threatening to the people of God than the threat that they would be left alone to face the harsh realities of history.

§ § § § § § §

The Message of Hosea 4–5

In these two chapters we have heard both the prophet and the Lord speak to a people caught up in false worship, to leaders who have lost their integrity and have made little more of religion than a way to make a living, and to nations who cannot see God at work in history. Through it all the prophet seeks to secure repentance; God seeks repentance and a genuine return to the ways of God's choosing. What can we learn from these chapters?

§ Following unworthy teachers has tragic results.

§ Sins are both by omission and commission; we either neglect to do what ought to be done, or we deliberately do what we ought not do.

§ Social morality and theological beliefs are intertwined.

§ There is an ecology to sin; when God's will is broken, the entire creation suffers.

§ Preoccupation with sensual thinking prevents wisdom.

§ God seeks wholehearted commitment to God's purposes.

§ Doing religious things is not necessarily the same as wholehearted commitment to God.

§ War between brothers is both sin and judgment.

§ God can and will work in history in order to secure commitment to God's purpose.

§ Without the assurance of God's presence in history, we are left with little more than our own resources to deal with the terrors and realities of history.

§ With God's presence we can endure history's best and worst.

§ § § § § § §

Hosea 6–8

Introduction to These Chapters

The catastrophe and tragedy of unsuccessful warfare brings the nation to an awareness for repentance. In this sense, the people should see the relationship between the events of history and their relationship with God. However, the depth of awareness is shallow. After a brief period of repentance, the awful depth of national sin is reemphasized. Israel not only continues turning from God. Israel runs the peril of losing its identity altogether as the people of God. A death sentence cannot be far removed from apostasy and loss of identity.

Here is an outline of chapters 6–8.
  I. Shallow Repentance and Intrigue (6:1–7:7)
      A. A litany of repentance (6:1-3)
      B. God rejects shallow repentance (6:4-6)
      C. Varieties of faithlessness (6:7–7:2)
      D. The kings have fallen (7:3-7)
 II. Israel Loses Its Identity (7:8-16)
III. Israel's Death Sentence (8:1-14)

A Litany of Repentance (6:1-3)

This section takes the worship/liturgical form of a song of penitence. While the song gives witness to trust in God, the tone of the song is far too confident to be authentic and sincere. A true repentance has an appropriate stutter to it. Israel's sin is far greater than

Israel realizes. The time required for penitence is much longer than one or two days. The people do not yet understand what is at stake (see 5:4). True repentance is much more demanding and difficult than just another religious ritual.

One of the central elements of Hosea's work is the hope for return, or turning to God (the verb meaning *return* is used in 3:5; 8:13; and 9:3). This means much more than a change in direction. It carries in it the notion of turning on oneself, an authentic confession and conversion. In the New Testament, Jesus' parable of the prodigal son (Luke 15) presents just such a turning. Hosea should be thought of as an evangelical preacher who offers hope for repentance. Unlike Amos, Hosea holds up great hope before his people. Real change is possible.

At no point in this short song is national sin mentioned. The worshipers assume that God's intention seems to be fulfilled by Israel's existence. A blithe confidence taints the repentance and reveals its shallowness. The people are certain that God's action is as regular as seasonal rains. They do not yet see that God's work is dependent upon a moral behavior and attitude among people.

Under no circumstances should the allusion to *two days* be construed as a reference to the images of resurrection. The saying is repeated here by the prophet to illustrate the remarkably callow and presumptive attitude of Israel.

God Rejects Shallow Repentance (6:4-6)

In verse 4, God addresses both Ephraim and Judah, that is, all the people of Israel. The word that is used is *love*. In Hebrew the word is *hesed*, or steadfast love. Here Israel's love is characterized as temporary, and as elusive as morning dew or mist.

God had attempted many times to speak to the people through both individuals (prophets) and the events of history. The prophets were not only the writing prophets, but men like Elijah (see 1 Kings 18). Another central element in Hosea's work is the intention of God for justice (*mishpat*). We have no exact equivalent in English for the Hebrew term *mishpat*. The justice and judgment of God's intent has to do with right relationships between individuals and God as a part of the covenant relationship.

In verse 6, God states the expectations of the covenant relationship. Against the false piety and ritual of the cult as well as the superficial notion that God will inevitably work on behalf of the people, God claims steadfast love (*hesed*) and knowledge of God, that is, a life of obedience and service, as central to the covenant.

Varieties of Faithlessness (6:7–7:2)

In this oracle God speaks of the diverse ways people have been faithless. *Adam* may mean one of three things. It could be a reference to the Genesis narrative in which the first human beings sinned. It could also be a reference to humankind in general. A third possibility is that it refers to a specific location (see Joshua 3:16).

Gilead may be a well-known center of political maneuvering.

Shechem has long been known for its importance in the covenant tradition (see Joshua 8:30-35. All of Joshua 24 presents a narrative of the covenant renewal at this location).

Israel suggests corporate and widespread guilt. Hosea speaks to the nation, not to specific individuals.

Horrible thing means apostasy.

The inclusion of Judah in this oracle (see verse 11) may be a contribution by an editor at a later time. Other sections of Hosea indicate similar possibilities of additions (see 1:7; 3:5; 4:15; 5:5). The possibility of additions by a later writer should not be interpreted to detract from the authority of the entire work. The later editor simply wanted to make certain that his readers would not overlook the reality of God's claim on all people at all times. God's claim was not merely a temporary or peculiar expectation of the people of the Northern Kingdom.

Harvest is a common image for the time when God will have the final act of history. The meaning is quite clear: Judah will have its time of judgment as well.

According to verse 11*b*, even in the midst of judgment and the final harvest, God speaks of *my people*. God still yearns to heal, that is, redeem, Israel.

God would heal, or redeem, if only the people of Israel would understand their need. Samaria is the capital city of the Northern Kingdom, also called Israel. But the syncretism with Baalism has blinded the chosen people to their sin. Tragically, the people have become so accustomed to the religious attitudes and behaviors native to the land of Canaan that they have lost the keen moral sensitivity that characterizes true biblical/covenant faith. But God remembers the covenant and sees a people who are in abject moral decay.

The Kings Have Fallen (7:3-7)

Even the rulers are morally bankrupt. This oracle was first uttered during a period of utter chaos. Assassination paved the way to power, unscrupulous nobility conspired, morality sank to new depths of depravity. The time was one of "every man for himself."

According to verses 4-6, conspiracy and intrigue had already reached the intensity of a furnace. The timing of the coup depended upon the leaders who were drunk to the point of illness (see 1 Kings 16:8-14).

Even in the most arduous of circumstances, leadership refused to repent and seek God (verse 7). Even though the nation suffered through the assassinations of four kings in a dozen years, they refused to repent.

Israel Loses Its Identity (7:8-16)

Throughout history the people of God have had to wrestle with the issue of identity. How can the people of God retain their distinctive identity while at the same time remaining a part of the larger and surrounding cultural and sociological forces?

In ancient times bread was baked first on one side and then turned. The allusion is to bread baked to a charred burn on one side yet still raw on the other. The image shows a half-fed people and a half-lived religion.

In verses 9-10 images of old age are used to describe Israel's failing strength. But even now, Israel remains stubbornly ignorant of its plight.

In verse 11 Israel is compared to a silly dove. Among the people, virtue has long since evaporated; single-hearted faith has disappeared. First Israel appealed to the nation of its historical memory that was powerful (Egypt), and then to the current threat (Assyria). In either event the result would have to be the same: war and ignominious defeat.

According to verse 12, as a fowler captures birds, so God will ensnare Israel in the realities of history.

A woe oracle introduces both accusation (13-16a) and punishment (16b). Once God has decided to act, there is no help for the rebellious people.

Verses 13-14 make the point that God intends to redeem but is unable to, because the people have rejected God's overtures. The people have tried to seek God through the rituals of Baalism. They are cutting themselves with knives in order to evoke response of the Baals (see also 1 Kings 18:28).

Forgetting about what God has done throughout its history, Israel sought to make alliances with foreign nations, thus rejecting God (verse 15).

According to verse 16, the irony is that when Israel seeks alliances the alliances themselves will prove to be Israel's defeat. Even the military leaders will suffer death.

Israel's Death Sentence (8:1-14)

This oracle begins a new section of oracles. Once again the oracle begins with a blast on the warning trumpet (recall the sequence of 5:8–6:6 where Hosea's work takes its cue from the Syro-Ephraimitic war).

Vulture or *eagle* is a metaphor often used to describe an encroaching enemy (see Jeremiah 4:13; 48:40; Lamentations 4:19; Habakkuk 1:8). The expression also captures the awful chaos that threatens to undo Israel from within. The *house of the LORD* means the land of Israel. Almost incredulously God characterizes the people: First they break the law and then they appeal to the God of the law/covenant! The verdict is obvious. The nation has rejected God. Ruin will overtake the people.

The development of the monarchy was never a universally accepted phenomenon in Israel's history. Even at the outset Samuel cautioned the people about the liability and peril of monarchy. Hosea concurs with that historical judgment in verse 4. The king and the cult are both machinations of the people. The dreadful history of the era showed clearly that the throne was achieved only through assassination and political intrigue. This attitude and behavior carry within themselves the seeds of their own destruction (see verse 7). Idols of course had been forbidden from the very outset of the covenant relationship with God (see Exodus 20:3-6; 34:17). Hosea suggests that both the monarchy and idolatry are on the same level of guilt since they are mentioned together.

Calf alludes to the image of a bull used in Canaanite worship (see 1 Kings 12:28-30). *Samaria* refers both to the capital as well as the citizens of the city. The result of Israel's idolatry is that both the idols and the nation will be splintered. History will vindicate the prophet's insight.

Verse 7 consists of two wisdom sayings. The first one would probably have been well known. It may well have been an observation as to what had been happening to the political fortunes of kings and usurpers of the throne.

The second refers to the devastation that will inevitably accompany defeat at the hands of the victorious empire.

The oracle in verses 8-10 condemns Israel for seeking alliances and making disastrous concessions. Again, Hosea addresses the loss of unique identity among other nations (recall 5:13-14; see 7:8-12). The oracle begins with a lament that already some of the land had been absorbed by the victorious Assyrians. In 733 B.C. both Galilee and Gilead had been overwhelmed and subjugated. King Hoshea had approached the Assyrians with a large tribute in a misplaced attempt to avert disaster. The results are quite clear. Contrary to Israel's political hopes, there will come a time when the people will not be ruled by their own kings.

In the oracle in verses 11-13, God addresses the evils of cultic worship. Altars are mentioned frequently in the Scriptures (see Genesis 12:7; 33:20; 35:7). In each of these instances, the altar is the spontaneous expression of thanksgiving. The altar reminds people of the presence and activity of God. Here, however, God rejects altars since they have become places of activity that is nowhere near the expectations of God for the covenant people.

The mention of written laws in verses 12-13 gives evidence that the people knew of a written form of the law, or Torah, at this time. Over against the requirements for a moral people in the Torah, the people have become enamored with sacrifice in and of itself. The punishment for violating the covenant is a return to the era of servitude in Egypt under oppressors (recall the allusion to the wilderness experience in 2:14-16). In fact, some of the people of Israel did find their way to Egypt when the nation was finally overwhelmed by Assyria.

In verse 14, the oracle concludes with an indictment of Israel's faithlessness. Rather than depending on God (the *Maker*), the people have built fortifications and walled cities. *Fire* means God's wrath.

§ § § § § § §

The Message of Hosea 6–8

Chapters 6 through 8 treat the political collapse of Israel. With the sounds and sights of destruction and chaos, and the threat of lost national identity, Hosea graphically captures Israel's dilemma. But even though God intends to use history as a means by which to punish Israel, still the same God holds out hope. The people may still return. They cannot return through shallow, ritualistic rites of sacrifice and memorized litanies. They can only return through a thoroughgoing repentance and confession to God.

What can we learn from these chapters?

§ Sin has its awful consequences (7:9).

§ The consequences of sin are not arbitrary; they are the natural outcome of given actions.

§ God seeks and desires heartfelt and sincere repentance that is more than mere ritual. True repentance is a deep and ethical process.

§ Any nation will decline when its leaders are morally corrupt.

§ In large measure we will become like those with whom we associate.

§ Identity once lost is very difficult to regain.

§ While external enemies may pose a threat, any individual or nation must beware the peril of internal chaos, discord, and sinfulness that will destroy as well.

§ God desires a right attitude and behavior rather than religious activity.

§ § § § § § §

Hosea 9:1–11:11

Introduction to These Chapters

Hosea continues the indictment of the nation of Israel for its apostasy, evidenced by its crass worship rituals and its profligate sensuality. Though the people are convinced that their cultic worship makes a difference, Hosea presses home his truth. There can be no legitimate worship unless it is worship of the God of the covenant. Since the prophecies stress the widespread and active cultic worship, they were probably first uttered in a time of relative peace, perhaps after the events of 733 B.C.

However, against the backdrop of continued national apostasy that warrants all the punishment God can bring to bear on Israel, Hosea addresses a profound theological question. His argument in part echoes Amos's argument that since the nation violated the covenant, the nation deserves just punishment. The law of God demands just consequences.

But what of the love of God? Surely the Hebrew people remembered God's love in the Exodus, in the wilderness, and in the period of the conquest. But is the love of God equal to the sinfulness of the people? Hosea dares to address this question in chapter 11 through the sensitive and powerful images of the father and his wayward son.

Here is an outline of Hosea 9:1–11:11.

From Celebration to Grief (9:1-6)

The description of the celebration indicates the feast of Tabernacles or Booths, that is, the festival of the harvest (see Leviticus 23:39-43; Deuteronomy 16:13-15; Judges 21:19-21). Hosea interrupts the celebration taking place, perhaps in one of the important shrines. One can only wonder what the people must have thought of this prophet interrupting one of the major festivals of Hebrew life. Where they had long since lost moral sensitivity to the sin of apostasy, Hosea's blood runs hot upon seeing yet another manifestation of the nation's evil. The people concentrate on the harvest, and thus on the fertility of the earth, rather than on their God and the covenant relationship.

Hosea returns to the graphic image of the harlot (recall 1:2-3). The wages of *a prostitute* refers to the payment given to the cultic prostitute (see Deuteronomy 23:18; Micah 1:7).

Threshing floors were frequently used for celebrations. See 2 Samuel 24:18-25, which tells of the celebration on the threshing floor of Araunah the Jebusite. The site later became the site of Solomon's Temple. First Kings 22:10 presents the sight of the kings of both Israel and Judah seated together at the threshing floor near the entrance to the gate of Samaria.

The land of *the* LORD (verse 3) asserts the truth that the land is not the people's nor does it belong to the Baals; it is the possession of God (see Leviticus 25:23, *the land is mine; you are but aliens and tenants* [NRSV] *with me*). Hosea alludes to the catastrophic effects of exile, including for some a return to Egypt (see 7:16; 8:13; 11:5, 11).

In verse 4, the prophet announces a time when the entire cult will come to an end. In Numbers 15:1-12 elaborate instructions are given for offerings. Included in those rituals are wine drinking. Hosea sees a time when all such celebratory libations will cease. Since there will be no shrines, sacrifices will cease; and the people will be defiled, that is, unclean.

The *festival of the* LORD (verse 5) is central to Hebrew life; without it the people would lose a major celebration (see Judges 21:19). Hosea lets loose with a terribly final assertion. The nation will be divided up into those going into exile (to Assyria) and those who will eventually be buried in Memphis, the capital of Lower Egypt and a city known for its graveyards. The once-sacred places will be overgrown by weeds. Desolation and death are serious threats.

A Fool for God's Sake (9:7-9)

In contrast to the situation with Jeremiah and Amos, we have no direct evidence as to how the people reacted to the prophet's word. We can surmise that his voice was a minority voice. The vast majority of the nation had succumbed to the luxuries and excesses of sensual worship. Their sensitivity to moral issues had been corrupted through lust. The single courageous voice of the prophet must have sounded either foolish or insane. Truth is often perceived initially by a minority of people. These verses do give what may be a glimpse of the peoples' response.

The prophet is a fool. Worse yet, he is considered by some to be a madman (see 1 Samuel 21:12-15; 2 Kings 9:11; Jeremiah 29:26). The only evidence we have of the people's reaction is what the prophet quotes from their responses.

Verse 8 is difficult to translate, as the Hebrew text is corrupt. The image may allude to the burden of the watchman's responsibility in Israel's history (see Isaiah 56:10; Ezekiel 3:17; especially Ezekiel 33:1-6).

In the days of the Judges a particularly gruesome episode occurred in Gibeah. An unnamed concubine from Bethlehem was violated, abused, and finally killed. Her owner then dismembered her and sent her remains to the various tribes of Israel. The entire episode is characterized by saying, *Has such a thing ever happened since the day that the Israelites came up from the land of Egypt until this day?* (NRSV) (see Judges 19:1-30).

A Deadly Attraction (9:10-17)

The nation continues its inevitable course from lust through corruption to utter decay. Recall that Hosea had already warned that a spirit of harlotry takes away an individual's brains. Sheer licentiousness yields its rewards whether in Hebrew or Christian tradition: death.

In verse 16 Hosea alludes to the years of first love—the wilderness years. Hosea pictures the past in images of perfection and ideals. No generation has ever lived in the golden age. The golden age is always one lived before the present era. Ba'al-peor is mentioned in Numbers 25:1-18. Peor was a cultic center in the territory of Moab. One characteristic of cultic worship was, of course, sexual fertility rites that were utterly opposed to God's covenant expectations.

In verse 11 Hosea works backward from birth. Not only will there be no birth; there will not even be pregnancy or conception at all. Barrenness will characterize Israel.

Even if, by some fluke, children are born, they will become victims of war. God will leave the people alone to face the horrors of history (recall 5:15). Warfare is never restricted to the fighting soldier. Families, women and children, young and old are caught up in its fearful excesses. The prophet is a student of history.

The anguished prophet interrupts his utterance in verse 14. He can do nothing other than pray for his beloved people. His prayer itself is interrupted. What would he have asked for? Without revealing his innermost thoughts, the prayer continues with the request for no more children to suffer, no mothers to either grieve for their slaughtered sons or be ripped open in pregnancy by marauding soldiers (see Amos 1:13).

Gilgal is the location in which Saul was made the first king in Israel (see 1 Samuel 11:14-15). It is also a location with a cultic worship center (see Amos 4:4; 5:5). Leaders are especially condemned for their poor leadership.

The oracle concludes with the prophet's reemphasizing the threat of an absent God. The once-proud nation will become little more than a group of desperate refugees wandering homeless in foreign nations.

Life Without King or Cult (10:1-8)

Once again the prophet addresses both puppet kings and puppet gods. The people still cannot understand the extent to which they have forsaken the covenant relationship with God. The more the earth yielded, the more the people thought that the cultic rituals of sexual orgy and idol worship had caused the blessing to occur (recall 8:11).

Pillars (verse 1 NRSV; NIV = *sacred stones*) are part of the cultic worship objects (see Exodus 23:24). Verse 2 shows God's reversal of the blessing.

According to verses 3-4, one of the central elements of national life, the monarchy, will be eliminated. Presumably the people themselves will recognize the futility of any king's efforts, hollow words, sham agreements or covenants, and false judgments, if the nation has refused to heed God.

The cult will perish. In verse 5 Hosea again alludes to the image of a bull in Bethel. Beth-aven is a derogatory reference to the cultic center. Hosea's description portrays a desperate people led by equally desperate priests attempting to make the idol do something in the face of Assyrian error. The idol itself will be carried into oblivion. In what may be an allusion to the final days of Israel in 722 B.C. with subsequent deportation of Israel's people, Hosea pictures the nation tossed about as a stick on flood waters.

Prominent heights frequently had cultic shrines on them (see 4:11-14).

All that is left for the people to do is pray for a natural catastrophe, an earthquake, to bury them alive before they have to endure the agonies of religious frustration and national collapse. Finally they will acknowledge their impotence.

Israel's Iniquity (10:9-15)

This oracle begins with judgment and indictment. It concludes with the announcement of a verdict. Gibeah is now more than a specific historical incident (recall 9:9; Judges 19). It now represents an attitude and a way of behaving.

In verses 11-13 Hosea draws on agricultural imagery. The animal has been trained to work but was allowed freedom to eat. Since the nation did not discipline itself, it will be disciplined by outside forces. Clearly Hosea envisions the hardships of exile. The discipline of work will be addressed to the purposes God has in mind. Again, the purposes are oft-repeated truths in Hosea's work: righteousness, steadfast love, and seeking the Lord through the law (Torah) instead of vapid cultic ritual. God will not return as the seasons do (recall 6:3). God's returned favor and salvation come as the result of authentic repentance and seeking.

In verses 13-15, the prophet makes the point that trust in the might of the military is a sin against God. Verse 13 could be an allusion to the ill-advised courage of King Hoshea in breaking away from Assyria (see 2 Kings 17:4). We have no other reference to the demand made by Shalman. However, it is certain that the original hearers knew of the disaster. All citizens of the nation, from the weakest to the strongest, will suffer terribly in the storm. Any nation that lives by the sword will die by the sword (see Matthew 26:52).

The Love of God (11:1-11)

How can any people survive if all they have is the haunting specter of an absent God who has abandoned them to the horrors of history? In one sense, the law of God has been justly fulfilled. The people have sinned grievously. Now they suffer the only appropriate punishment. God's patience has worn through. Now God acts through history to execute the just punishment. But in another sense, Hosea cannot leave the issue alone. Is God's love equal to the demand of the law? Modern readers need to see the incredible courage of Hosea in asking such an important question. In the Christian tradition the question finds its sharpest expression in the paradox of the crucifixion. There, on the height of Golgotha, the love and law of God came to their inevitable collision.

Hosea portrays God in the person of a loving father. The oracle recovers the love of God from Israel's historical memory in verses 1-4; pictures the present love of God in verses 5-7; appropriates the love of God in the present suffering in verses 8-9; and finally portrays God's love in the future in verse 11.

Father is a powerful image. God had been described as the father of the tribe (Exodus 4:22; Isaiah 1:2; Jeremiah

3:19, 22). God's love stirred God's saving act in the Exodus from Egypt. But the nation quickly turned from God in rebellion. One can hear the heartbrokenness of God in the review of history. Hosea uses the word *heal* to describe God's saving acts in history. The connection between God and Israel is historical and moral. The relationship was conferred by love. It should have been confirmed by maintenance of covenant responsibility. Hosea is unafraid to picture God with very human feelings, sympathies, and gentleness.

The present crisis (described in verses 5-7) reflects either actual refugees or a political policy of seeking alliances with the enemy. Some kind of a military disaster has already occurred. Hosea may be referring to the Assyrian campaign of 733 B.C. But even with the facts of history and current events facing them with bare truth, still the people stubbornly refuse to repent.

Hosea then portrays God expressing to Israel/Ephraim God's own tortured soul. *Admah* and *Zeboiim* are towns that had been totally destroyed along with Sodom and Gomorrah (Genesis 10:19; 14:2, 8). In God's own soul wrath gives way to compassion. There follows a triple denial of wrath's finality. *I will not execute my fierce anger; I will not again destroy . . . I will not come in wrath.* God does have feelings like those of human beings. But God's action is utterly unlike human behavior. Hosea's words describe; but they do not define or limit God's action.

Verses 10-11, which describe a promised homecoming, may be additions by a later editor. They refer to the future in which God will restore to the land exiles who have languished in foreign lands. Under no circumstances can the return be the accomplishment of the exiles themselves. The return will be yet another gift of a gracious God.

§ § § § § § §

The Message of Hosea 9:1–11:11

The emotions of these chapters range from the white-hot wrath of a rejected God to the compassionate feelings of a loving father. The events range from the horrors of warfare waged on pregnant women and little children to the promise of a return to a beloved homeland. What can we learn from these chapters?

§ Blessings of harvest and bounty are from God.

§ Buildings and institutions do not endure; moral discernment and obedience to the covenant prevail.

§ The root of sin is lack of trust in God.

§ Exclusive trust in the power of military might is a sin against God.

§ Religious leaders have the obligation of prophetic ministry—declaring God's interpretation of events and moral expectations.

§ Sometimes the feeling of faith is less important than the execution of responsibility and duty to God.

§ History is God's workshop.

§ In Israel's history is the memory of God's loving action on behalf of all humanity.

§ God's relationship with people is both historic and moral.

§ God's own soul is torn by faithless people and nations.

§ § § § § § §

Hosea 11:12–14:9

Introduction to These Chapters

In the English translations, chapter 11 concludes with verse 12. In the Hebrew Scriptures chapter 12 begins with, *Ephraim has surrounded me with lies*. At this point we will follow the arrangement of the Hebrew Scriptures.

Following the touching image of a caring, compassionate father and the promise of a return home, the final section of Hosea once again utters a series of oracles that speak of Israel's evil and eventual doom. When the word of grace is finally spoken, it is a severe grace that emerges from God's love.

Here is an outline of chapters 12 through 14.
I. Israel's Evil and Doom (11:12–12:14)
  A. Israel at the Jabbok (11:12–12:6)
  B. Israel's crisis of identity (12:7-14)
II. Toward an Inexorable End (13:1-16)
  A. God against Israel (13:1-8)
  B. Israel's shattered illusions (13:9-16)
III. A Severe Grace (14:1-8)
IV. Instructions to the Reader (14:9)

Israel at the Jabbok (11:12–12:6)

Verse 12 can stand on its own as an independent unit. Since the verse includes a reference to Judah, some scholars suggest that this is yet another addition by a later editor. In this instance the editor contends that Judah is not guilty of the sin of deceit.

In 12:1 Hosea uses the metaphor of the dreaded *sirocco*, a seasonal wind that is scorchingly hot. It destroys vegetation with its searing winds sweeping in from the desert. The policy of seeking alliance with Assyria (see 2 Kings 17:3-4) is as elusive as trying to catch the wind.

As in earlier oracles, the court scene is established when an indictment is brought against Israel (see verse 2). Jacob is the twin brother born second, grasping his brother Esau's heel (see Genesis 25:26). Jacob is known as the supplanter, the cheat. Hosea contends that the nation Israel is much like its ancestral patriarch.

The allusion to the struggle is from Genesis 32:22-30. Hosea does not duplicate the narrative exactly. Through his allusion, however, he suggests that Jacob had not merely thought about God, he had attempted to overpower God in a personal encounter. In the context of Hosea's historical era, the nation through its military alliances and foreign intrigues still attempts to be more powerful than God's strength. Hosea's intent is clear. The descendants of Jacob will need to experience the reality of God and wrestle with their God as Jacob had. They too will learn through hard experience that as the individual's strength was not sufficient, neither is the descendant nation's strength sufficient.

Bethel became important to the patriarchs (see Genesis 28:11-19; 35:5-8). Later on in history it became one of the major sanctuaries. By Hosea's time it had achieved that major importance (see Amos 7:13).

Verse 5 sounds like something from a worship setting, perhaps a doxology.

In verse 6 God speaks to Jacob; Hosea uses the historical speech to speak to his contemporary listeners. Note that return is still a possibility. Any return, turning, or repentance is the result of a gracious God who has been gracious with the ancient fathers of long ago as well

HOSEA THROUGH JONAH

as the contemporary people of Israel. Hosea uses the opportunity to speak of central truths he has mentioned numerous times before: steadfast love and justice.

Israel's Crisis of Identity (12:7-14)

In this oracle, Ephraim/Israel is characterized as having adopted the same attitudes as the surrounding peoples. Israel has become like unscrupulous traders who use false weights. The higher calling of ethical sincerity of the covenant has been lost.

God speaks with a corrective identity in verse 9. God is the God of the Exodus who will reverse the salvation of the people. As before, the people will once again languish in servitude.

In verses 10-14 God continues to address the people. The word of God came through prophets, to whom God spoke personally and individually through visions and images. The true prophets of God employed the past in order to interpret the present. But the people ignored the prophets of God. Evidence of their disregard is in cultic worship. Here the current cultic actions in Gilead (recall 6:8) and Gilgal (recall 9:15) are condemned. Since the oracle does not clarify what the activities are, Hosea assumes that the people had knowledge of the cultic behavior and knew what they were doing. The result of God's judgment will be that the altars, once the pride and joy of cultic worship, will be little more than heaps of stones similar to what people would find in any field.

Verse 12 may be an addition by a later editor from Judah. In any event, the verse returns to the theme of the patriarchal tradition of Jacob which is related to Bethel (see Genesis 28:11-22). The land of Aram is Paddan-aram (see Genesis 25:20) to the northeast of Palestine in Syria.

In verse 13 Hosea returns to the dominant theme of this oracle: the prophetic heritage of Israel. Moses is the prophet par excellence. In order to resolve the crisis of identity Israel needs to recall its prophetic heritage and the Mosaic covenant.

However, in response to the powerful imagery of prophetic heritage, Israel refuses to adopt its historic identity (verse 14). This leaves God little option. God must execute judgment and punishment on sin that is equivalent to bloodguiltiness, that is, sin that warrants the death sentence.

God Against Israel (13:1-8)

Tragically, the people of Israel refused their highest calling to be the people and nation of covenant loyalty and ethics. Utterly refusing to consider either the pathos of God the compassionate father or the scathing indictment of a people who have lost their identity, the nation will now face its inevitable punishment.

An oracle of judgment opens the chapter. Verse 1 deals with the past glory and strength of Israel. Verse 2 characterizes the people's current sinfulness through despised cultic worship of sacrifice and idolatry. Verse 3 predicts a grim verdict for the future through events in nature that disappear very quickly: morning mist before the rising sun, chaff that is blown away by the wind during threshing, or smoke escaping from a humble home.

In the oracle in verses 4-8, God begins speaking of the gracious actions God has taken in history. The first and primary saving act of God is the Exodus from Egypt. It was God who chose Israel in the first place (see Exodus 20:3; Deuteronomy 6:5). The people should know that only God can save the nation. None of the other supposed powers can help the nation; not kings (13:10), not military might (14:3), not idols (13:2; 14:3).

But after all of God's saving activity, the people turned to Baalism and Canaanite worship, forgetting their God altogether. The inclination to forget was recognized by the writer of Deuteronomy since many correctives are repeated there: 6:10-19; 8:11-20; and 11:5-6 are all admonitions not to forget the gift-giver when Israel comes into possession of the land.

According to verses 7-8, God will become a curse like marauding animals to Israel (see 5:14; also Leviticus 26:22; Jeremiah 5:6).

Israel's Shattered Illusions (13:9-16)

In verse 10 Hosea makes the point that God has historically saved and protected the chosen people. Only with God's saving action did Israel come into being, survive the threat of extinction at the Sea of Reeds, endure the tribulations of the wilderness, and conquer the territory of Canaan. But all of that would not guarantee continuous grace. Israel's sin has to be punished. This oracle may be in response to the people protesting against the dire predictions of Hosea.

Evidently the people have called attention to the institution of the monarchy (see 1 Samuel 8:6), an institution that God had not wanted in the first place, that had been the source of hope. In response to these cries the prophet has only scorn. *Where now is your king that he may save you?*

In verses 12-16 Hosea presents his final and most crushing verdict of doom.

The image of storage (verse 12) is taken from papyrus wrapped up (see Isaiah 8:16; Jeremiah 32:10). Israel's guilt is assumed.

According to verse 13, years that might have been filled with the hopes of birth and life will be filled with death. Hosea unflinchingly uses graphic images of a fetus refusing to be born. Labor pains are often used as metaphors for writhing in judgment (see Isaiah 26:17; 13:8; Jeremiah 13:21; 22:23). Even through the worst of circumstances, God holds out the possibility that renewal can occur. But Israel cannot see the possibilities.

Interpretations of the divine oracle in verse 14 vary.

Are the statements questions or are they assertions? In the New Testament, Paul interprets them as messages of salvation (see 1 Corinthians 15:55). The tone of the oracle is one of judgment. To be sure, death and Sheol represent a serious danger. It appears that for the moment God will refrain from the warranted and appropriate punishment.

In verses 15-16, using the image of the scorching sirocco Hosea shows how God's intention will be carried out. Assyria is the wind from the East (see 12:1). The horrors of military disaster will be the plague and death announced by God.

All will suffer from the Assyrian terror. The Assyrians were notorious for their cruelty. In 2 Kings 15:16 a gruesome atrocity is recorded: *he ripped open all the pregnant women*. Amos refers to the same sort of crime against humanity (Amos 1:13).

A Severe Grace (14:1-8)

After the prediction of utter destruction, Hosea returns to the blessed hope that with God the gates of repentance are always open (see Isaiah 55:6-9). Once again the prophet returns to one of the predominant themes of his work: *turn/return* (in Hebrew, *shuv*). For Hosea the possibility of return always remains open, even at the crashing conclusion of the dreaded judgment.

Hosea says that Israel has *stumbled* (recall 5:5).

In verse 2 the people are instructed to speak. This section may be a part of a larger liturgical tradition of repentance. In the earlier entreaty (recall 5:5–6:6), the peoples' speaking was superficial, revealing how unaware they were of the depth of sin and the desperate need for real repentance. In sharp contrast, this prayer has the sound of authentic recognition of human sinfulness and the sufficiency for help that is God's and God's alone.

In the prayer in verse 3, Israel recognizes the futility of seeking alliances with foreign nations, especially Assyria (see 5:13; 7:11; 8:9; 12:1). Even the most sophisticated of military weaponry (chariots) will not save the nation. Israel at long last will forsake idolatry.

According to verses 4-7, through the trial of defeat and exile God will once again choose to love Israel and heal (see 5:13; 6:1; 7:1) the broken and bruised nation. Earlier the prophet had seen the dreadful possibility that even the chosen people could reject the love of God once too often. Hosea had dared envision a moment when the love of God could be spurned. This sin against love could bring only one result: God would abandon the people to the uncertainties of history (see 5:15). However, here at the conclusion of his work, the prophet presents the gracious insight of the victory of love over sin.

The same God who refuses to compel love will not be forced to love. God chooses to love the nation.

In verse 7 the image of shadow is used as metaphor for God's protection (see Psalms 17:8; 36:7; 121:5). Israel once knew a time of remarkable blessing and fruitful abundance; God will bring Israel a fruitful life again.

This oracle concludes in verse 8 with the unique image of the fir tree. In no other place in the Hebrew Scriptures is God referred to by using this metaphor. Hosea has strained throughout his work to tell Israel of God's unique role in Israel's life. Through God alone comes salvation and blessing. As the prophetic symphony comes to its conclusion, the theme is once again sounded: *It is I who answer and look after you.* From Hosea, Israel learns that love is the ultimate element in true religion.

Instructions to the Reader (14:9)

This verse is clearly a later addition that serves as both an evaluation of the book as well as instruction for future generations. Both the style and content of the instruction are from the wisdom tradition (see Proverbs 4:11-12 and Ecclesiastes 12:9-14).

§ § § § § § §

The Message of Hosea 11:12–14:9

Hosea wrestled long and hard with the apparent paradox between the love and law of God. If the law is paramount then love must be secondary. If love is primary then what is to be done with the law's requirements? Hosea dared to present a God whose heart is tortured by the sinfulness of the nation. Yet, the same God cannot forever turn away from the beloved people. Only due to God's own steadfast love can the people hope for a future. What can we learn from these chapters?

§ The love of God overcomes all sin, even the sin of rejecting God's love.

§ Genuine repentance is always demanded, and always possible.

§ God will go to great lengths seeking and redeeming people.

§ Salvation comes from God alone.

§ God is not a tradition, but a reality with whom all people must wrestle and come to terms.

§ The courageous words of the prophet are worthy of our consideration; history has vindicated the prophet.

§ § § § § § §

Introduction to Joel

The book of Joel consists of 72 verses divided, in English Bibles, into three chapters. In the Hebrew Scriptures, the book is divided into four chapters with 2:28-32 as chapter 3 and 3:1-21 as chapter 4. The immediate cause for the book is a devastating plague of locusts that threatens to destroy the land and the economy. As with other prophets, Joel takes his cue from real events in the life of the nation. He goes further than the event by interpreting the importance or the meaning of the event to his contemporaries. For Joel the overwhelming swarms of locusts suggest not only an act of God, but also the future activity of God in the life of the nation.

Joel, the Man

We know very little about Joel himself. His name, meaning *Yahweh is God*, is not an unusual name, as it occurs elsewhere in the Old Testament (for example, 1 Samuel 8:2; Ezra 10:43). He is the son of Pethuel. His home may have been in the territory traditionally associated with Reuben (see 1 Chronicles 5:4).

Joel is familiar with worship procedures and priests, and himself may well have been what is called a Temple prophet. In this sense he shares similar views with Haggai and Zechariah. He shows a familiarity with Jerusalem and the surrounding country.

Date of the Writing

One of the critical questions in interpreting Joel has to do with the date of his writing. He could be assigned to one of two periods. Since some of his words are parallels with other prophets (some 20 verses), either those prophets quoted from him, or he quoted from them. Since there is no mention of national sins that would warrant punishment from God and no mention of large menacing empires (neither Assyria nor Babylon is mentioned), scholars conclude that Joel's work comes at a relatively late time. At least one allusion is to scattered people (3:2), thus implying the Exile as an historical era already past. Therefore, we may date his work sometime during the time period of the fifth century B.C.

The Message of Joel

A careful reading of Joel suggests that the prophet does not blithely cast aside the rich traditions of his predecessors. Rather, he takes their work and reinterprets it for the present moment. Joel stands at a vital moment when the old traditions of the prophets were giving way to the newer apocalyptic thinking. In large measure, he reinterprets the traditional prophetic message with a new freshness for his listeners. Joel seeks the meaning of a current crisis while at the same time straining to see the horizon of God's future. Just as Joel would not arbitrarily do away with tradition, he would not eliminate formal worship services.

One of the central elements in Joel's work is the *Day of the* LORD, mentioned no fewer than five times (see 1:15; 2:1, 11, 31; 3:14). No one can escape from its inevitable disaster. But there is still room for hope, since the opportunity for repentance is always present. God's intention is not merely judgment and punishment, because God always yearns for repentance and acknowledgement by the chosen people.

Joel 1:1–2:11

Introduction to These Chapters

Chapter 1 and the first eleven verses of chapter 2 provide a fitting introduction to the prophecies of Joel. In this material, the crisis that the people of Israel were enduring in Joel's day is described in detail.

The material may be outlined as follows.
  I. Title (1:1)
 II. A Call for National Lament (1:2-14)
III. A Terrible Crisis (1:15-20)
 IV. The Day of the LORD (2:1-11)

Title (1:1)

The word of the LORD (see Hosea 1:1; Micah 1:1; Zephaniah 1:1) comes to the prophet. The prophet begins with the statement of his authority. The utterance that he brings to the people is not of his own design, nor does it emerge solely from his own imagination. The message has divine authority.

Pethuel is found only here in the entire Old Testament. The name may be a variation of *Bethuel,* which is mentioned in Genesis 22:22-23.

A Call for National Lament (1:2-14)

The prophecy begins with a summons to hear an instruction. An event of unparalleled magnitude has broken loose. The summons includes old men, thus implying that even in memory, including the memory of the grandparents, nothing of this sort has happened. The crisis is of such proportions that children will tell their grandchildren about it.

In one graphic verse (verse 4), the prophet tells what the crisis is: a terrible locust plague. The description includes four stages of the pest's life cycle: cutting, swarming, hopping, and destroying. The image is of successive waves of the insects devouring everything. Verses 5-14 make the point that the overwhelming plague is a national disaster that will affect every element of society. In response to the emergency, the nation is summoned to lament.

In the first stanza of the summons (verses 5-7), Joel addresses the first class of people who will feel the effects of the locusts. People dependent upon alcohol will suffer since the grape vines will be destroyed. Others who are not necessarily as dependent as alcoholics will have to pay much higher prices since the supply will be severely restricted. Note that Joel does not seem to mind using very graphic imagery and illustrations taken from every level of society.

The image of *lions' teeth* shows the immensely destructive power of the locusts. The devastation is complete; even trees are denuded.

The second stanza (verses 8-10) implies a formal worship setting with well-known patterns of worship. *Sackcloth* signifies penitence (see verse 13; Amos 8:10). The intended audience may have been the citizens of Jerusalem. The *grain* and *drink* offerings are part of the normal daily sacrifice (see Numbers 28:3-8). Again the prophet tells of the magnitude of the event. In the Scriptures the ground has feelings (see Isaiah 33:9). Grain, wine, and olive oil are primary agricultural products.

Another element of society is addressed in verses 11-12. The farmers are the next class to mourn. As with the earlier description (verse 4), the repetition of strong verbs emphasizes the utter destruction taking place. Verses 10-12 may imply a corresponding drought taking place (see also verses 17 and 20).

Priests, who are addressed in verses 13-14, are the last class to whom the prophet issues the summons. Since the priests are addressed, most scholars conclude that Joel was himself not a priest. In what appears to be a customary practice, the priests are instructed to gird themselves in sackcloth, to lament, and to wail for the entire night in the sanctuary (see 2 Samuel 12:16 where David spends an entire night lamenting the sick child born of his tryst with Uriah's wife Bathsheba).

Ministers of (NRSV; NIV = *minister before*) *my God* are the men who serve in the inner court of the sanctuary (see Ezekiel 43:18-27). Joel uses the very personal expression *my God*. To *sanctify* means to set apart and designate with religious rites. The *fast* is a sign of national repentance (see 1 Samuel 7:6; Jeremiah 36:6; Jonah 3:5). The fact that all the inhabitants can be gathered for this event implies the existence of a relatively small population and thus a post-exilic community in Jerusalem. The entire summons reaches its climax when the gathered are *instructed* to *cry to the* LORD.

A Terrible Crisis (1:15-20)

In verse 15 Joel sounds the keynote for his entire prophecy. The Lord is quite near, inescapably near. Perhaps the prophet is correcting a popularly held notion that God is somehow far off. Had worship become merely a rote routine of ritual and sacrifice? No other sins are enumerated. Nor is there any suggestion of exile from the land, or of captivity. Later on (2:13) Joel will return to a criticism of religion that had turned into rending garments instead of hearts. Joel's use of the word *destruction* in addition to referring to the natural disaster also implies *El Shaddai*. This term means *Devastator*, or

Destroyer in Hebrew, and is another name for God in the Scriptures.

The Day of the LORD occurs five times in Joel. Three times it is used against Israel (1:15; 2:1, 11); twice it is used against other nations (2:31; 3:14). The term means a time, not necessarily a specific day, of God's judgment. For the balance of the work this topic will dominate Joel's prophecy.

The effect of the unavoidable day is the cessation of any joy and gladness (verse 16). During the dreadful crisis all celebration will be impossible. With some imagination one can hear the prophet preaching and evoking from his listeners a spontaneous response.

In verses 17-18 Joel again emphasizes the extent of the devastation, with the sad image of cattle wandering aimlessly in a vain search for food and water. In the Hebrew Scriptures even the beasts of the earth and the earth itself suffer as a result of sin committed by humanity (see Genesis 3:17-18; Jeremiah 12:4 indicates that the ground itself is dismayed).

Fire and *flame* (verses 19-20) are metaphors for either the destruction caused by the locusts or of a drought that occurs at the same time (see Jeremiah 9:9-10; Amos 7:4). The *wilderness* (NRSV) is pasture land, not necessarily the arid and barren wastes of the Negeb. Note that again the beasts join the lament.

The Day of the LORD (2:1-11)

God issues terse instructions: *Sound the alarm* (see Jeremiah 4:5; Hosea 5:8; 8:1). Joel draws on the common sight of watchtowers scattered throughout the nation. The responsibility of the watchman was to sound the alarm in case of any danger. Perhaps one of the best allusions to this practice is in Ezekiel 33:2-4, where that prophet is instructed by God to sound the alarm to Israel. In Joel's prophecy the ram's horn, the *shofar*, often used to announce holy days or summon the people to worship (see Revelation 8:6-13), is to be sounded now as a startling blast.

Zion is a sacred high place in Jerusalem on which special revelation occurs. Mount Zion had for centuries been a part of the hope that Jerusalem itself would remain secure even in the midst of war (see Obadiah 16-17).

The description of the day of the Lord in verse 2 is one of *darkness and gloom*, not unlike other manifestations of God in the past (see Exodus 10:22 where Moses causes darkness and gloom to appear; Deuteronomy 4:11 describes how God is revealed to the Israelites as darkness and gloom). The manifestation of God's presence with Israel is called a *theophany*. Joel does not necessarily have to present new or fresh material. His genius is a reworking of traditional material with fresh meaning and insight.

Joel describes the plague of locusts in language similar to the account of the plague against Egypt (see Exodus 10:14-15). However, in the past God worked on behalf of Israel. In the current crisis God works against Israel.

In verses 3-5, using the language of theophany (see Exodus 24:17; Zephaniah 1:1), Joel continues the vivid description of the locusts' destruction as a manifestation of God's destructive wrath. In an ironic reversal, the creation goes from being an Eden-like garden to a barren wasteland. From this horrendous event no one can escape (see Isaiah 2:10-21; 13:14-16; Ezekiel 30:6-9; Amos 5:18-20). Contrary to deep human desires Joel presents a critical theological insight. The human being wants, almost desperately, to have a God who can be controlled. No, people would not say so in as many words. But the impulse is always present to restrict or limit God to certain actions and behaviors based upon the attitude and action of the believer. Joel will have nothing to do with that sort of thinking. No one will escape the ravages of God's action. Furthermore, God has the freedom and authority to change blessing into curse.

The imagery is from a military invasion; the event is still the overwhelming catastrophe of the swarming locusts. Revelation 9:7-10 is based on this graphic image. Joel increases the impact of the event with the cacophony of sound accompanying the tumult.

In the midst of all of this, Joel pictures the people suffering unimaginable anguish with their faces gone ashen due to the horror of devastation (see verse 6). Another prophet, Nahum, also describes ashen-faced people (see Nahum 2:10).

After glancing at the people and noting their reaction, Joel returns to the sights and sounds of the invasion (verses 7-14).

Earlier Joel showed the beasts and the earth suffering as a result of the day; now even the cosmos is affected by the event (verses 10-11; see Judges 5:4; Isaiah 13:10, 13). The locust plague is nothing less than God's own means by which to reach the people. Traditionally God's instruments had been other peoples (see Isaiah 10:5-10 in which Assyria is the *rod of* God's *anger*. Joel takes the tradition of agents sent by God and dares to picture insects as the agents. Joel's creative genius characterizes the prophet's ability to look beyond the natural event and to see in it much more than natural catastrophe. One of the central tasks of prophetic ministry is to interpret for people what may not be obvious. For Joel the locust invasion is a message of God's intention from God's own self.

The oracle concludes with the only question left to the people. One can almost hear it blurted out, *Who can endure this day*? Joel adds the descriptive words *great* and *dreadful* (NIV; NRSV = *terrible*) to augment the already vivid and horrible day. Joel has drawn the drama to a high tension. How can the people endure?

§ § § § § § §

The Message of Joel 1:1–2:11

Modern readers may find the graphic imagery and the theological considerations to be terribly outdated or even offensive. Few of us consider natural catastrophe the direct result of a deliberate decision and action by God. Seldom do we hear people even attempt such conclusions. But for the ancient Israelites, the realms of nature and human experience are both within the power and authority of the eternal God. Joel's insight into the larger issues of the time cannot be disregarded. If we are inclined to discount or to scoff at anyone who would see the action of God in natural events, we would be on the way to wisdom when we understand as well that God's creation, all of it, has running through it a moral direction and intention. We ought not scoff at those who see God at work through natural events; they see God caring for them and vitally concerned and personally involved in their lives.

What else can we learn from reading these verses?

§ Even prophetic religion at times respects the need for external expressions of worship (1:9, 13-14).

§ Disasters or catastrophes can serve to turn people toward God.

§ God can use disaster to speak to people.

§ In the face of overwhelming and uncontrollable natural events, we become aware of our utter dependence upon God.

§ God's intentions are for all people.

§ God is not far removed from human history; God is near and involved.

§ § § § § § §

Joel 2:12–3:21

Introduction to These Chapters

The previous section ended with the anguished cry, *Who can endure the day of the LORD?* Other outbursts may have included, *How much longer?* The people ache for resolution from their present distress. Popular religion frequently takes its cue only from the natural calamity or stress of the moment. We are in no manner surprised by the national outburst of lament.

As far as the majority of citizens are concerned, the catastrophe is the problem. But for the prophet, the stress of the moment is only the beginning. Joel refuses to speak only to what is apparent or obvious, while he will continue with his concern for the present crisis. Joel uses the idea of day of the Lord to develop an enlarged notion of a future hope. Joel's task is to appropriate faith equal to the demand of the hour and build a faith of sufficient depth for eternity.

Here is an outline of Joel 2:12–3:21.
  I. Call for National Repentance (2:12-17)
 II. The Promise of Fertility (2:18-27)
III. The Outpouring of the Spirit (2:28-32)
 IV. God's Judgment of Oppressors (3:1-21)

Call for National Repentance (2:12-17)

In response to the anguished cry *who can endure*, Joel speaks of legitimate and authentic hope.

A new section begins with 2:12. Previously, a summons had gone out for a national lamentation. We can assume that the worshipers gathered and that the priests carried out their assigned tasks. However, the forms and ritual of worship are not sufficient. Acting out religion is not the same as a thoroughgoing moral commitment to the purposes and intentions of God. Joel now directs national attention to the purposes of God as much as averting the disaster of the locust plague.

The oracle opens in verse 12 with the divine oracle formula in which God adds an invitation to repentance. Repentance is possible only because of the graciousness of God. The initiative is always with God. Perhaps Joel sees a people who are convinced that the quality of their repentance will be enough to stave the threat. Repentance, however, takes its cue not from the people but rather from the very character of God. God yearns urgently for people to return to God's ways. The gates of repentance are always open.

The invitation to return is deeply rooted in tradition (see Deuteronomy 30:9-10; 1 Samuel 7:3; 1 Kings 8:48-51; Amos 4:6-11). In Amos the invitation consists of three parts: a promise, an accusation, and a threat. In Joel's oracle only the promise is stated.

In what is perhaps the best known verse in the book, verse 13, Joel summarizes the summons. The observance of religious ritual is not sufficient. The heart is the source of moral strength. God desires a total reorientation of an individual's life so that the intentions of God become a paramount motive and direction.

Tearing of clothes is a traditional expression of anguish.

Using traditional language (see Exodus 34:6; Psalm 86:15), Joel characterizes the God of Israel as *gracious, merciful* (NRSV; NIV = *compassionate*), slow to anger, and *abounding in steadfast love.*

Even with a return to God following the outward

expressions of worship and public lament, still God is free to make God's decision. At least a part of the human religious impulse since time immemorial is to consider the action of religious observance of any kind as binding on God. A fair amount of modern Christianity, especially in the Protestant tradition in the United States, tends toward the notion that an action on our part in some sense obligates God's benediction. Joel's caution, therefore, should be well taken. We have no way of knowing for certain whether or not God will choose to change God's mind or to bless the people.

The threat of the locusts poses much more than an immediate threat of their harvests and momentary unpleasantness. Indeed, the plague threatens the very existence of the nation as an economic and social entity. Previously the people had been concerned primarily with their worship. Now they confronted the very real possibility that the entire nation could literally be eaten up or dried up. Joel could hardly have stated the need more emphatically. Joel performs a great service by subtly calling attention to the sheer grace of God that allows nations generally, and Israel/Judah in particular, to exist.

The second stanza of this oracle (verses 15-16) concerns instructions to the priests and ministers. As instructions in 1:13-14 followed the summons in 1:5-12, here too specific instructions are given. *Sanctify* (NRSV; NIV = *consecrate*) means to prepare for a solemn event. The entire community, with no exception, is to gather.

According to verse 17, the priests' appropriate position is between the vestibule and the altar (see 1 Kings 6:3). Once in place, the priests are to speak the lament. Earlier (1:13-19) Joel had led the prayer. Here the priests themselves are to speak.

The Promise of Fertility (2:18-27)

From this point to the end of the work, all prophecies have to do with the future. Recall that the people gathered for worship uncertain as to whether or not God would choose to change God's mind.

Following the lament comes a divine oracle that indicates God has heard the prayer (verse 18). The prayer will be answered (see 1 Samuel 7:9; 2 Chronicles 20; Psalm 12:5). Joel does not mean to imply that the peoples' repentance caused God's change of heart. The choice is still God's to make.

Jealous also carries with it the notion of zeal (see Deuteronomy 4:24).

God's response in verse 19 is that the disaster described in 1:10 will be reversed. What was once lush, now destroyed, will once again be green and fruitful. God will intervene so that foreign nations will not ridicule Israel any longer.

Reference to the *northern army* (verse 20) is ambiguous. What exactly does Joel mean? Traditionally, enemies arose from the north (see Jeremiah 1:14-15). The allusion may not be to an historical event at all, but to the very real and present threat of the locust invasion. In either event, God promises that the threat will not come again. The *eastern sea* is the Dead Sea; the *western sea* is the Mediterranean. The images of once-proud soldiers, now dead and rotting in the desert sun, complete the military allusion. Evidently the haughtiness of the once-proud evoked God's action.

In the prophet's oracle in verses 21-27, the prophet gets to announce the reversal of the awful news that he had had to deliver earlier (recall 1:15-20). As the beasts groaned and suffered earlier, here they rejoice along with the people. To the prophet, rain and harvest are not merely physical benefits, but religious sacraments. They are signs that God has returned to the people and that God's zeal is again on their behalf. Early rains came in November; late rains from March to April.

The blessing of God will reverse the catastrophe of 1:2–2:17. Moreover, the terrible losses will be made up; God will restore the locust years.

Whereas the people have suffered terrible privation and great hunger, in the future they will have plenty to eat. In sheer gratitude the people will erupt into thanksgiving.

A strong word follows in verse 27. None of God's action is to be taken as a matter of fact. Along with the blessing of God comes the attendant requirement to acknowledge God as one who manifests self through the giving of gifts—the covenant God who has expectations of the covenant people (see Deuteronomy 5:29), and who is the only God.

The Outpouring of the Spirit (2:28-32)

Doubtless a large percentage of the population fairly exploded with praise and thanksgiving at the announcement of a blessed future. Equally true is the fact that individuals must have basic physical and material benefits before they can begin to think of any religion of a higher order. Joel's arrangement of his material suggests that he has an understanding of this basic necessity. But the prophet is not content to allow for the religion to remain at a basic or physical/material level. His hope stretches beyond the restoration of the land and the survival of institutions of religion, the Temple and formal worship with attendant hierarchies, to a higher gift, the gift of the Spirit.

God's manifestation in the midst of Israel has not yet reached its climax. The promise of 2:27 is about to be fulfilled to an almost inexpressible degree. The Hebrew word for *Spirit* is the same word as for *wind* (*ruach*). In the Genesis narrative of the Creation, the Hebrew reads a very suggestive, "God breathed the *ruach* into the human being." The word *Spirit* therefore implies something about life itself being a gift of God (see Psalm 104:29-30; Isaiah 42:5).

The Spirit of God is bestowed upon people who have special functions to perform (see Judges 6:34, which tells of Gideon being controlled by the Spirit). In Jeremiah

51:11 it is God's Spirit that stirs up kings to historic undertakings.

Only with the presence of the Spirit will the people be able to understand how the current judgment and crisis make sense. Evidently Joel lived during a time when prophecy itself was relatively rare. In that context he anticipates one manifestation of the presence of the Spirit as prophecy.

Dreams and visions have always been considered legitimate channels of revelation. In Genesis 28:12-17 Jacob dreams of the ladder reaching from earth to heaven. The Lord speaks to him, *I am the* LORD, *the God of Abraham your father and the God of Isaac; the land on which you lie I will give to you and to your offspring* (NRSV). In Jeremiah 23:25-32 the Lord condemns those who claim to have dreamed dreams of prophecy but who really have not. Joseph had the gift of interpreting dreams. Recall his lifesaving interpretations while imprisoned.

In addition to understanding and the gift of prophecy, God's Spirit will bring about social changes. All distinctions—sex, age, class or social position —will be neutral. In the Christian tradition this hope finds expression in Paul's daring assertion in Galatians 3:28: *There is neither Jew nor Greek, slave nor free, male nor female* . . . (NIV; NRSV = *flesh*).

The phrase *all people*, when read in conjunction with *in the midst of Israel* suggests that the Spirit will be God's gift to Israel, not the entire creation. From the Christian perspective, of course, the implication is that the Spirit will indeed be for the entire creation. However, in Genesis the promise of blessing is directed to the entire creation (see Genesis 12:3), and in the prophetic tradition the entire creation is likewise promised. Isaiah echoes this hope when he says, *In days to come the mountain of the* LORDS *house shall be established as the highest of the mountains, and shall be raised above the hills; all the nations shall stream to it* (Isaiah 2:2).

God's Judgment of Oppressors (3:1-21)

At long last Judah, that group of oppressed people who have known the horrors of military disaster and collapse, exile and bitter natural disaster, will see the judgment of other nations. Finally God will vindicate the faith of the beleaguered minority.

In those days (see Jeremiah 33:15; 50:4) means a period of restoration (see Ezekiel 39:25; Zephaniah 3:20).

The *valley of Jehoshaphat* (verse 2) has at its root the Hebrew word *shaphat* (to judge). Many interpreters identify this valley as the Kidron valley. However, this place is not mentioned anywhere else in the Old Testament. In any case, the real point of Joel's argument is not the location but the *purpose* of the gathering. Other nations will be judged for the scattering of God's people through deportation and exile, the dividing up of God's land, and their crimes against humanity, particularly the cruelty of selling prisoners of war. Not even the children of the defeated were treated benevolently.

Verses 4-8 contain oracles of judgment against Tyre, Sidon, and Philistia. Deeply-felt animosity and historical hatred wells up. God's rhetorical question does not seek an answer. Instead God intends to speak a word of judgment on the offending nations. Clearly the nations have justified to themselves their reprehensible actions throughout history. Tyre, one of the major cities of the Phoenicians, is modern day *Sur* (see Isaiah 23; Ezekiel 26:1–28:19; Amos 1:9-10; Zechariah 9:2-3). Sidon (see Ezekiel 28:20-26; Zechariah 9:2) is modern day *Seda*, some twenty miles north of Tyre. Philistia is also mentioned in Isaiah 14:29-31; Jeremiah 47; Ezekiel 25:15-17. Philistines had been known for their wanton plundering (see 2 Chronicles 21:16-17). The charge against the offending nations is wholesale plunder both of official treasures of the Temple and of the land of a defeated Israel.

Slave trade is a particularly onerous charge (see Amos 1:6). *Sabeans* were slave traders from Arabia.

Nowhere else in the Old Testament are the former oppressed to be found as executers of God's own judgment and punishment. The punishment for the offending nations will be in kind for what they have done to others. All of this is authenticated by nothing less than the Lord's own speaking and intention.

In verses 9-12, foreign nations are summoned to a final battle. With broadly stated irony God reverses prophetic hopes of an end to warfare. In both Isaiah's and Micah's hope weapons of war are fashioned into instruments of peace and tranquility (compare Isaiah 2:4; Micah 4:3). The braggarts will prove to be the weakest of the lot. In a taunting tone God intends to elicit hasty response by foreign powers.

Through agricultural images Joel indicates that the day of the Lord is imminent (verses 13-17). *Harvest* is often used as a metaphor for the final judgment (see Isaiah 17:5; Matthew 9:38; Revelation 14:14-20).

Joel draws on an awareness that the ancient Israelites would have had that we do not have. The scene of treading grapes would have been one of great noise and celebration (see Isaiah 16:10; Jeremiah 25:30; 48:33). Joel immediately shifts to the shouts and noise of battle. The linking element is the mingled sounds of shouting and noise. The Day of the Lord, the Day of Judgment that had been narrowly missed by Jerusalem, now begins. The descriptive words tumble from the prophet's mouth. The utter chaos of the moment makes any specific description impossible. What Joel does is to create a feeling for the dreadful end that has begun for Israel's historic enemies.

Even as the sounds of the chaos of battle fill the air, Joel interrupts the description with a fond hope and an affirmation of faith. Even now God is the strength and salvation of Israel.

At long last the holy city of Jerusalem will be the Lord's own tabernacle (verses 16-17; see also Isaiah 1:24-28; 52:1; Zechariah 8:3; Revelation 21:2-27). More importantly, for Joel the goal for which God yearns most earnestly is recognition and acknowledgment by the people that God is God. From the first sound of the first invading locust to the cacophony of the final battle against the nations, God has yearned to be known as God by the people of God's own choosing. Though agriculture be destroyed, economies destroyed, formal institutions of worship threatened, and national existence itself endangered, through the blessings of God's own spirit to all and through the final defeat of longstanding hostilities, God yearns to be known as God.

Verses 18-21 contain an assurance and an interpretation. The exaggerated picture of Israel's future appears to be a later addition to Joel's original work. The images are much more akin to apocalyptic images than to traditional prophetic metaphors.

The terrible effects of the crisis in 2:19-26 are to be reversed, according to verse 18. In place of arid wasteland the region will be almost unbelievably fertile (see Amos 9:13). Wadis, river beds that may engorge with a flash flood but usually are dry, will become constantly filled and life-giving streams (see Ezekiel 47:1-12).

Verse 19 presents a stark contrast to the fertility of Israel—the desolation that will characterize both Egypt (see Ezekiel 29:9) and Edom (see Ezekiel 35:3-4, 7, 14-15). Edom is an especially evil people who will experience the punishment of God (see Obadiah 6-16).

According to verses 20-21 the chosen people, the survivors and their descendants, will live peacefully in Jerusalem, the holy city. Joel's work concludes with the assurance of God's presence and a promised vengeance on the enemies of God's people. God and God alone is the source of all blessings, from agriculture to life to history and the future.

§ § § § § § §

The Message of Joel 2:12–3:21

Joel did not interpret the current crisis solely within

the context of life's usual demands and expectations. He cast the entire catastrophe within the bounds of God's eternal—both historical and future—purposes. He appropriated much existing prophetic and national liturgical material. In this sense he was certainly not original. However, he shows remarkable skill at reinterpreting traditional material in order to give his people courage for today and hope for tomorrow. What else can we learn from Joel?

§ Judgment day will be both blessing and curse.

§ What judgment day means depends to some degree upon the attitude and faith of the individual.

§ God seeks genuine repentance and not a mere using of religion for immediate ends.

§ God yearns for the transformation of God's people into morally sensitive and historically aware people.

§ God's spirit is equally available to all, regardless of the distinctions of age, sex, or social/economic class.

§ No people, no nation, will escape the judgment of God.

§ God, while recognizing and accepting the institutions of religion and worship, is not satisfied with external form.

§ A crisis can be used to transform an individual toward the intentions of the eternal.

§ § § § § § §

Introduction to Amos

The prophet Amos is the third of the minor prophets in
the canon. Chronologically, however, he is the first of the
writing prophets. His work occurs during the long and
prosperous reign of Jeroboam II, around 786–746 B.C.

In other prophetic works, the sights of military
collapse, natural catastrophe, economic disaster, and
foreign intrigue all fill the imagination. Amos ministered
during a time remarkably free from external stress. Other
prophets have to make sense of disaster, both natural and
political. Amos found himself speaking an urgent word
to a complacent people long since grown spiritually
flabby and morally insensitive. A sensitive reader can
hear the groans of the oppressed, the flippancy of vested
interest, and the anguished cries of men and women
caught up in a corrupt court without hope. We can even
hear the voice of God raging against a nation
prematurely confident in the false security of ritual and
arrogantly ignorant of the divine will of God. Power and
wealth, luxury and licentiousness yield abuses of justice,
oppression of the poor, corruption of the innocent, and
an intolerance for spiritual forces.

The people to whom Amos addresses his work are a
prideful people (6:13-14) and a comfortable people with
abundant wealth (3:15; 5:11; 6:4-6). Sinfulness is not
restricted to the male population. Women too are
addicted to wine (4:1). In a morally insensitive society
injustice prevails, but it takes the prophet to name the sin
for what it is. The poor are oppressed, sold into slavery

(2:6-9; 5:11), and have no recourse through the legal system because the judges themselves are as corrupt as the surrounding culture (5:12).

The tragedy is that even though the prophet speaks, entrenched and vested interests will adamantly ignore the divine will for the nation (7:10-14). The discerning prophet speaks a word from God to a people who have lost the sensitivity to the demands of God for their personal and corporate lives. They were willed with optimism. The prophet discerns the moral truth in a time when popular dogma refused to heed anything of the higher calling.

Amos speaks a harsh word against a cold people. Nothing in his work throbs with hope that the nation will repent and, in doing so, save itself. For Amos the requirement of God's law is quite clear: inescapable punishment.

The task would have been sufficient to test anyone's mettle even if the work had been done by personal choice. But Amos, like other individuals summoned by God into God's work, was summoned against his will and quite without his asking for the responsibility. However, Amos felt overwhelmed by the reality of God and the urgency as well as the immediacy of God's will for Israel. He could do nothing else but obey (3:8). The result of his faithfulness is the utterance and compilation of this great prophetic work of social justice.

Amos 1–2

Introduction to These Chapters

The first two chapters of the book of Amos contain biographical information about the prophet, as well as the first few in a series of oracles delivered against foreign nations.

These two chapters may be outlined as follows.
I. Title (1:1-2)
II. Oracles Against the Nations (1:3–2:16)
    A. An oracle against Damascus (1:3-5)
    B. An oracle against Gaza (1:6-8)
    C. An oracle against Tyre (1:9-10)
    D. An oracle against Edom (1:11-12)
    E. An oracle against the Ammonites (1:13-15)
    F. An oracle against Moab (2:1-3)
    G. An oracle against Judah (2:4-5)
    H. An oracle against Israel (2:6-16)

Title (1:1-2)

Amos's prophecy begins with Amos's *words*. Other prophetic works begin with words spoken by the Lord. Amos makes his living as a sheep breeder (see also 7:14). His home territory is the rugged area of Tekoa to the south of Jerusalem. In the solitude of the rugged wilderness, Amos is able to reflect on the life of his people without the interferences of urban life. In the wilderness he also learns the disciplines of paying close attention to the subtle sounds that would reveal danger. Without the distractions of city life, Amos could brood over the intention of God for the nation.

Uzziah ruled over the southern kingdom of Judah, Amos's nation, from 783 to 741 B.C. Even though Amos resides in Judah, he still speaks to the northern nation of Israel. Unlike most other prophets, Amos will actually travel to the place to which his prophetic oracles are addressed.

The words of the Lord are so powerful that Amos can see them (see also Isaiah 2:1; Micah 1:1).

Doubtless the earthquake to which Amos alludes would have been familiar to the original hearers. However, the actual date of the event cannot be determined.

Mount Zion is the highest elevation in Jerusalem. Traditionally the greatest revelations occur on this height.

To the prophet, *word* meant a good deal more than merely an utterance. In Hebrew the term for *word* means *deed* as well. Spoken words took on the character of something actually being done; an event had occurred. Recall that in the earliest narratives of Genesis, God utters a Word and the Creation happens. Later in the patriarchal narratives Isaac speaks the word of blessing to the scheming and cheating Jacob. Even though the blessing had been gained by ruse, Isaac could not retract the spoken word of blessing. The blessing had already been given.

The imagery of melting snows and scorched pasture land evokes memories of dreaded disasters. The Israelites would not consign the disaster to the realm of natural events caused by flukes of seasons or untoward combinations of weather patterns. In the Hebrew mind events are caused by no less than the word of God. When God speaks, something happens.

The word of the Lord which causes nature to take its course is the same word that has power to direct history for the purposes of blessing and curse, salvation and judgment.

Oracles Against the Nations (1:3–2:16)

The oracles of 1:3–2:16 are directed against foreign nations as well as the two kingdoms of God's chosen people. Each of these oracles contains the same parts. The five parts are: the messenger formula, a proclamation of judgment, specific indictments or charges, punishment, and a concluding formula.

The messenger formula, *Thus says the* LORD (NRSV; NIV = *This is what the* LORD *says*), initiates the prophetic oracle. The prophet has been overwhelmed by the reality of God. His own personality is never completely lost; each prophet has a discernible personality evident in his work. But the ego seems to have been overcome by God. The prophet speaks for the eternal. Through the messenger formula the authority of the utterance is firmly established. The message is from God.

A proclamation of judgment follows. There can be no doubting the inevitability of punishment. When God's law or intention has been violated, the offending party will be held accountable.

Judgment is rarely stated in broad categories. Specific indictments or charges are listed. We may be able to distill moral principles from the prophet's utterances; the prophet indicates very specific crimes or sins committed by the offending individual or nation.

A specific punishment will be meted out upon the offending party. The punishment will be inevitable and inescapable.

The oracle concludes with a variation of the messenger formula, *says the* LORD. This formula recalls the authority behind the utterance and confirms the utterance as true.

Amos begins his oracles by pointing toward the wrongs committed by foreign nations. The technique he uses is a very clever one. With some imagination the modern reader can picture the listeners hearing these words for the first time. Amos starts with detested foreigners who had done horrendous wrong. Without a doubt the listeners nod assent and find themselves emotionally caught up in the argument. Those evildoers need to be punished. Like a good preacher, Amos establishes a good cadence in his speaking. He involves the congregation. There may be an occasional "Amen." As he builds his case he weakens their guard. Caught up in emotional and moral outrage, the people of Israel cry out against the evil nations. Carefully the prophet urges them on. Finally he levels the charges against the people of Israel themselves. Almost without realizing it, they have acknowledged their own sin.

An Oracle Against Damascus (1:3-5)

Damascus is the capital city of the kingdom of Syria to the northeast of Israel. Isaiah too speaks against the Syrian capital (Isaiah 17:1-3). A later prophet, Zechariah, speaks against the same city (Zechariah 9:1-3). The collection of evidence illustrates how deeply rooted are Israel's anger and hatred.

For three sins (NIV; NRSV = *transgressions*) . . . *and for four* is a means by which to demonstrate the severity of the wrong that has been committed.

Amos begins his work by pointing to the blatant crimes of neighboring nations in order to impress upon the people the truth of God's claim on all people, not merely on the people of Israel. Even though those others may not acknowledge God to be the Lord, and though they do not obey even the most minor of ethical principles, God is still God and has a moral claim on them. In Amos's thinking, moral principles are at work in the universe. These principles impinge on all peoples.

The crimes of which Damascus and other states are guilty are violations of basic ethics of human decency in wartime. Amos's prophecy differs from other prophets who bring ethical insights of the highest order. Micah's passionate hope for an end to war, . . . *they shall beat their swords into plowshares, and their spears into pruning hooks; nation shall not lift up sword against nation, neither shall they learn war any more* (Micah 4:3) finds no echo in Amos. Isaiah's deep insight into the nature of vicarious suffering in the servant songs (Isaiah 42:1-4; 49:1-6; 50:4-9; 52:13–53:12) is absent from Amos. Amos does not introduce a new ethic into his prophecy. He draws upon what would have been very familiar material from Israel's own history. One of the narratives to which Amos alludes describes the excess of violence against an unnamed concubine during the period of the Judges. Such excesses had been unacceptable for generations.

Amos employs agricultural imagery. The threshing sledge was dragged over grain in order to separate the grain from the stalk. With the advent of advanced technology, iron made the machine much more efficient. Amos's reference may mean that the iron-toothed machine was used to crush and maul prisoners of war after a battle in the village of Gilead in the Transjordan. Battles with neighboring Gileadites were common (see Judges 12:1-6).

Hazael and *Ben-hadad III* were rulers of Syria (see 2 Kings 13:3).

Ancient cities were fortified by massive walls. Access to the city was restricted to large gates. The story is told that during the period of the Judges Samson, with his enormous strength, seized the gates of Gaza and took them to the crest of a hill (Judges 16:1-3). The gates were secured by means of a heavy iron bar. In this oracle Amos asserts that the security of the city will be broken by God.

Valley of Aven may also be read *Valley of On*. It was located near a range of mountains in Lebanon.

Beth-eden means *house of paradise* or perhaps *house of pleasure*. The site was near the Euphrates River.

Kir is the place from which Arameans or Syrians

originated (see Amos 9:7). This oracle's context suggests that the conquered peoples will be exiled.

An Oracle Against Gaza (1:6-8)

Gaza is not only an area, but could possibly be the name of a major Philistine city. The crime for which Gaza will be punished is the selling of prisoners of war as slaves to Edom. Seizing captives and making them slaves was a very common occurrence. However, selling the unfortunate people as mere commodities with little more than economic value violates the humanity of those individuals.

Three other cities will be destroyed by fire: Ashdod, Ashkelon, and Edron.

An Oracle Against Tyre (1:9-10)

Tyre was the leading port city of Phoenicia. The crime for which Tyre will be punished is that of delivering refugees for deportation. Amos's understanding is that the refugees were kin through covenant relationship to the Phoenicians. Relationships through the covenant were as binding as family relationships.

Tyre will suffer the same fate as Gaza: fire.

An Oracle Against Edom (1:11-12)

Israel had a long tradition of conflict with the territory of Edom. In the earliest years of Israel's history David defeated the Edomites and established garrisons in the land (see 2 Samuel 8:13-14). David's son Solomon had to contend with uprisings led by the Edomite ruler Hadad (see 1 Kings 11:14-15). The prophet Obadiah speaks of Judah's bitter experience at the hands of a gloating Edomite people.

Since this oracle alludes to the action during the collapse of Jerusalem (Ezekiel 35:5-6; Obadiah), scholars conclude that this is a later addition. In any event, the

Edomites relished their hatred and animosity. They kept the ill feelings festering over the course of many years.

Teman and *Bozrah* are both cities and regions in Edomite territory.

An Oracle Against the Ammonites (1:13-15)

The crime for which the Ammonites will be punished is the atrocity of ripping open pregnant women. The crime is one of wanton violence enacted against both those living and those yet unborn. Crimes of this sort, though terribly cruel and gruesome, were not unusual. In 2 Kings 8:12 a man of God weeps upon viewing the terrible crime. When Menahem sacked Tappuah, pregnant women were disemboweled.

For quite some time the territory including Gilead was disputed territory (see 2 Kings 14:25, 28). Gilead is the area known in tradition as having been settled by Ephraim.

Rabbah, modern day Amman, Jordan, was the capital city of the Ammonites.

The punishment for the Ammonites and their leaders is defeat and deportation into exile.

An Oracle Against Moab (2:1-3)

The territory of the Moabites is to the east of the southern half of the Dead Sea. The conflict and hatred between these adjacent territories of Moab and Edom have always been extremely harsh. Moab's crime is desecration of the dead. Evidently a king's remains had been exhumed and burned into lime. The lime could then have been used as a whitewash. The point is that what was once a human being had been completely dehumanized, even in death, to be little more than components of wall paint!

God will use fire to destroy the Moabite city of Kerioth. Both the population generally and the king specifically will suffer death.

Up to this point the oracles have been addressed to foreign nations that border on Judah and Israel. The crimes for which they are held guilty are crimes against humanity both living and dead, from the womb to the grave. Note that the actions are not crimes because they were perpetrated against God's chosen nation. They are crimes because they violate basic humanity.

An Oracle Against Judah (2:4-5)

Judah's sin is not an excess of war. Judah's sin is that the nation rejected the law (Torah) that is the teaching of God. In Hebrew the word for law is *torah*, and it means much more than a set of written codes. A good translation of the term is *revelation*. Amos contends that, like the ancient fathers, the contemporaries pursue pagan gods. Judah will suffer by fire.

An Oracle Against Israel (2:6-16)

Once Israel's attention is raised by the brutal and blatant crimes of other nations, Amos articulates the more subtle crimes of Israel. Israel's crimes are not committed against foreigners. The crimes are perpetrated against Israel's own people: the poor of the nation. Since Amos knows more about his own people, the crimes are stated in much more specific detail.

People who were otherwise completely innocent were sold into slavery for little more than a small debt (verse 6). Debt slavery itself was not forbidden in Israel. Individuals could sell themselves. Exodus 21:2-11 lists detailed instructions for how slaves are to be purchased. Deuteronomy 15:12-18 includes the prescription of time limits to servitude. In Leviticus 25:39-46 limits are placed on what can be done with slaves. Amos's argument, therefore, is not against slavery. Rather, Amos's blood runs hot at the thought that people have been sold for little more than a song with no regard for their basic humanity. Amos is always concerned about maintaining essential human dignity even among the weakest members of society.

According to verse 7, in a land grown rich and luxurious, the wealthy have lost any sensitivity to the poor. The arrogant wealthy brutally oppress the poor.

Moral depravity prevails. A man and his son going in to the same maiden suggests a father using his son's wife for crude gratification of sexual fantasies. The expression may also allude to the practice of Temple or cult prostitutes.

Debtors have been exploited (verse 8). Even the basic necessities of life have been taken away from already unfortunate people.

Note that none of these charges against Israel is of a very high ethical norm. Each of them is woven into the fabric of Israel's tradition. What Amos has done is lift up from Israel's rich tradition the minimal expectations that God has for all the people.

In verses 9-12 Amos alludes to a time in Israel's history during which Israel herself was quite helpless. In earlier times God had acted on behalf of Israel when the Amorites, native occupants of Canaan, threatened to annihilate the invading Israelites. Amos evokes memories of an ancient mercy. The memories will serve to shame and convict Israel of her contemporary sin of mercilessness against the poor, the weak, and the helpless.

The *Nazirites* are individuals who have taken a specific set of vows. Included in the vows is an abstinence from alcohol.

In verses 13-16, an announcement of punishment, Amos cites an argument from history. As once God acted on behalf of the weaker Israel against the stronger Amorites, so God will again act on behalf of the weaker ones. This time, however, the weaker are in Israel itself, the poor and oppressed of the land.

Without the first mention or hint of hope for repentance, the punishment is announced with a prediction of subsequent behavior. Utter panic will engulf even the stoutest of warriors and seasoned of veterans. All of them will flee panic-stricken and naked.

§ § § § § § §

The Message of Amos 1–2

The first two chapters of Amos consist of oracles against sinful nations. Both crimes of war and crimes of social justice are judged as sinful. Without the sensitive insight and courageous word of the prophet, Israel may well have continued her blithe ignorance of the subtle crimes against her own people. What else can we learn from these chapters?

§ God has expectations of minimal levels of morality for all nations.

§ When God speaks events are put into motion; something happens.

§ No power can long stand when God decides to act against it.

§ God is at work in all nations' history.

§ When God needs a spokesperson, God will raise up a prophet.

§ God has a special concern for the poor of any land.

§ Prophets have to publicly reject popular dogma in order to present God's truth.

§ When we are inclined to neglect weaker members of society, we must remember God's compassion and mercy toward us in our own moments of weakness and need.

§ § § § § § §

Amos 3–4

Introduction to These Chapters

Amos's argument from history spanned the behavior of friend and foe alike. His prophecy has its source deeply rooted in God's moral character and purpose. Other prophets would have to wrestle with the meaning of national catastrophe (recall Joel's work with the locust plague and Hosea's work with the Assyrian crisis). Amos takes his cue from what transpires in Israel's own society and culture. Doubtless his listeners were offended by his daring inclusion of Israelites in the same sinful category as foreigners who had committed obviously cruel and violent acts against others. We can perceive anger and resistance since Amos subtly reveals conflict with opponents.

Here is an outline of these chapters:
  I. Peril and Privilege of Election (3:1-15)
    A. Election and responsibility (3:1-8)
    B. Judgment (3:9-11)
    C. A means of judgment (3:12-15)
  II. Oracles Against Israel's Excesses (4:1-13)
    A. An oracle against the women (4:1-3)
    B. An oracle against worship (4:4-5)
    C. An oracle about Israel's refusal (4:6-13)

Throughout her history Israel believed that God protected the chosen people in a special way. In Amos's day people clung to that belief. However, the popular notion was taken as matter of fact and quite irrespective of moral standards. In the following series of oracles, Amos now addresses the election of Israel not as privilege but as a burden of responsibility.

Peril and Privilege of Election (3:1-15)

Each of these sections begins with the same proclamation formula with the introductory phrase, *Hear this word* . . . (see 4:1; 5:1; also 7:16; 8:4).

Election and Responsibility (3:1-8)

Amos's argument is rooted in the history of Israel and God's dealing with the chosen people. As God is the God who saved Israel from slavery, so the same God has a moral claim on the Israel of Amos's day. The saving act by God carries with it an attendant moral expectation. Recall that the Decalogue, the Ten Commandments (Exodus 20:2-17), begins with God's statement, *I am the* LORD *your God, who brought you out of the land of Egypt, out of the house of bondage. You shall have no other gods before me.* God's claim is not a capricious one leveled against Israel for no purpose. God's claim comes from God's own righteousness as well as God's action on behalf of Israel. Here God's action is unique. Later on, Amos will picture God's saving act as a part of a larger history (9:7).

Verse 2 suggests that God has *known* (NRSV; NIV = *chosen*) only Israel. However, Amos makes references to other nations (see the oracles in chapters 1 and 2; see also 9:7). Therefore, the meaning of this verse is that God has known Israel in a special manner (see Exodus 19:4-6; Deuteronomy 7:6). By using the well-worn term, Amos may also be turning back on the people a religious mentality of exclusivity that had developed. What Israel is about to learn is that religion is not an escape from the realities of history and moral demand. Rather, true religion is an opportunity for both investment in history and lively witness through faithful execution of sensitive moral behavior.

In verses 3-8, the oracle continues with the prophet's justification of what is clearly an unwelcome critical word. In a subtle manner Amos reveals the resistance he feels from others about his work. Later he will have a sharp confrontation with a royal priest (7:10-14). Earlier Amos, or if not Amos then other prophets, had been told to be quiet (recall 2:12).

In imagery that draws on Amos's experience in the wilderness, the prophet illustrates the relationship between the prophet's words and the events of the time. In the wilderness, meetings are hardly by chance. An appointment must be made.

An animal of prey will not disclose its position by making noise. It will roar only when it has its prey cornered. A bird will not simply fall out of the air without a trap to ensnare it. Over and over Amos builds the imagery of cause and effect. First Samuel 5:1-12 is the narrative of what happened to the Philistines when they captured the ark of the covenant. Even they recognized that catastrophe has a cause behind it. From the idea of animals Amos evokes the image of a city in panic at the blast of the warning horn. Amos uses this image to move from metaphors from nature to a very real political/military threat that will crash upon the people.

Verses 6b and 7 shift the focus from the prophet himself to God. Thus the people's real problem is not with the prophet and his speaking. Their real problem is with God, whom they have offended.

In the Old Testament, God is revealed to chosen servants (Genesis 18:17-19; Exodus 4:15-16; Jeremiah 7:25).

In verse 8 Amos states his firm conviction that he must preach against the popular opinion. He is compelled to preach (see also 1 Corinthians 9:16).

Judgment (3:9-11)

The oracle in verses 9-11 is addressed to the citizens of Samaria, the capital city of Israel. God summons old and detested enemies, long since known for their cruelties and oppressions, to see the evil done by the people of God. The irony of Amos's assertion would sting the proud people.

The Lord's charge is that Israel has lost her moral sense. Worse yet, Israel itself has become a nation that stores up violence against its own people (see Jeremiah 6:7; 20:8; Ezekiel 45:9; Habakkuk 1:3).

A Means of Judgment (3:12-15)

Amos employs common illustrations with which all people would be familiar. The short saying in verse 12 is introduced by the messenger formula. As thoroughly as a sheep is mauled and devoured by a lion, so shall Israel be mauled and destroyed by the enemy (see Hosea 5:14; 13:7). From all the finery and architecture in which Israel's wealthy pride themselves, only pieces of furniture will survive the destruction. Amos offers no hope whatsoever for the nation.

In verses 13-15 Amos reaches far back into the ancient tradition of the patriarchs (Jacob—see 6:8; 7:2, 5; 8:7; Isaac—see 7:9, 16; Joseph—see 5:15) in identifying the people. Through these ancient traditions Amos reminds the people that they are not merely the citizens of a nation under the reign of Jeroboam II; they are an historically identified people.

On the day (verse 14) refers to the concept of the Day of the Lord, a time in which God will judge nations. The Day of the Lord is one in which Israel will rejoice because at long last Israel's enemies will be punished by God. A storm cloud of judgment now gathers over Israel. Two institutions in particular will be targets.

First, God will strike the sanctuary at Bethel (in Hebrew, *the house of God*). The altar, with its horns that had traditionally been a place of refuge, will be of no avail in avoiding the oncoming destruction. The altar will be rendered little more than broken bits.

Second, the luxurious homes of the wealthy will be destroyed. The wealthy wasted much money on building finer and finer homes (see 1 Kings 22:39 for another reference to ivory-inlaid homes), while the poor languished in debtors' prison and the land suffered the outrage of injustice. Amos employs an ironic pun when he speaks of the houses of the rich that the rich themselves obviously value more highly than their identity as the house of Jacob. Amos reveals his own tradition of the desert as well. In the rugged wilderness he had no use for the sophistication and outward show of fine homes. Amos has little good to say about the city.

Oracles Against Israel's Excesses (4:1-13)

In a new set of oracles Amos indicts Israel for its excesses. In each oracle a specific indictment is charged against specific elements of society. It is followed by an announcement of punishment.

An Oracle Against the Women (4:1-3)

The modern reader may consider calling any woman a cow to be sufficiently offensive as to require little else to be said. In this instance Amos is not pointing to their biological manifestations. He is instead alluding to Bashan, the finest pasture land in Israel. Animals grazing in this fertile area were the best and the most pampered (see Deuteronomy 32:14; Psalm 22:12; Ezekiel 39:18).

The charge contends that the women do not act publicly. They work behind the scenes controlling their husbands.

The description of the women's punishment in verses 2*b*-3 is not clear. Could the *hooks* be an allusion to the instruments used to drag lake beds to retrieve drowned victims? Perhaps the hooks refer to devices used to drag corpses from battlefields. The word may also imply the manner in which captives were restrained during the forced march into exile.

Mount Hermon is in the Bashan range of mountains.

Though there is some question about the specific meaning of *hooks*, the image is clear. The wealthy and influential women of the nation will suffer a fate equal to that now endured by the poor and oppressed.

An Oracle Against Worship (4:4-5)

In this short oracle, Amos seeks to expose the heart of Israel's religion. In so doing Amos takes on a formidable task. Not only will he show the hollowness of popular religion but also he will indict national religion. National or cultic religion had replaced authentic hope with a false security engendered by ceremony and ritual.

Religion itself is not the problem. Something deep inside the human spirit wants to erect an altar or utter praises in thanksgiving. Recall the Israelites' action upon safe passage through the Jordan River. Joshua ordered an altar to be built (see Joshua 4). Recall that Joel employed the institutions of religion, the sanctuary, priests, and a shared memory of liturgy, in order to steel the people to the present crisis.

Bethel has deep roots in Israel's religious and political traditions. In the earliest narratives of the ancient fathers is the one concerning Jacob's dream at Bethel. Genesis 28:10-19 tells of the flight of Jacob. While sleeping, he dreamed of angels ascending and descending a ladder. When he awoke he called the place *Bethel*. In Hebrew this means *the house of the* LORD. He built an altar there.

Much later in Israel's history, after the tragic civil war that erupted upon Solomon's death, the king of the northern kingdom of Israel realized the need for a sanctuary to which the faithful could make regular pilgrimages. Jeroboam I established the sanctuary in Bethel as a national sanctuary, to serve the same function as Jerusalem had in Judah, not available any longer to the people of Israel (see 1 Kings 12:28-33). This sanctuary became an important religious center for the entire kingdom, including the king's family (see Amos 7:13).

Gilgal too was the site of a very important shrine. Like Bethel it had a long tradition of national life. Saul had been anointed the first king of Israel here (see 1 Samuel 11:14-15).

Thus, in the earliest years of the nation's life, the highest motive of religion and the reality of national interest had become inextricably entwined. After generations of national religion, or cultic religion as it is generally called, Amos confronts the national religion and its practices with stinging sarcasm.

Using words that official priests would have used, Amos mockingly summons the worshipers to the sanctuaries. Amos continues by showing the shallowness of cultic worship. The people do not worship for the purpose of praising their God or of learning more of the intention of the eternal. Rather, their motive is to allay guilty consciences with public displays of rote ritual and long since vapid ceremony.

Sacrifice of animals was common (see Leviticus 3–5).

Pilgrims brought different kinds of offerings. Some were the standard tithe (see Deuteronomy 14:22-29). Others included thank offerings used in a ritual of praise (see Leviticus 7:12-15), and freewill offerings used sometimes as a peace offering (see Leviticus 7:16-17). But the ceremonies were little more than a sham. The people loved to go through the rituals. A religion that had been used to build a civilization and to preserve it will be hard pressed to sustain a keen edge of critical self-examination and monitoring of social issues.

National religion, with its vested interests, reduced God to a national god, confused God's dwelling with humankind with a location in a specific sanctuary, and correlated national interest with God's ultimate intentions. These crass developments outraged Amos's prophetic spirit. Doubtless Amos spoke a single voice or at best a minority stance. The majority of people would find his scathing indictment entirely unthinkable.

Their religion had turned into superstition. They sought their Lord through ritual and sacrifice at the shrine rather than through the stern disciplines of history and social responsibilities. Against the ritual of superstition Amos places the reality of history.

An Oracle About Israel's Refusal (4:6-13)

A recital of God's acts in history illustrates how frequently God attempted to reach the people. God had repeatedly sought response from the nation through natural catastrophe: famine, drought, crop failure, and blight. But Israel refused to heed God's summons. When natural calamity did not work, God employed the forces of history against Israel. The images Amos uses present a scene with which Israel was familiar: warfare and defeat of military forces with the tragic consequence of death hanging over the land.

Sodom and *Gomorrah* are always associated with evil. Here Amos includes Israel herself with the detested cities.

Note that religion itself is far from obviated. Indeed, official cultic religion went on at full intensity. The people loved their religion of ritual and ceremony (4:5). But the people had lost their moral sense.

The only conclusion that God can draw from the abysmal record of stubborn Israel is that punishment is necessary (verse 12). The words used to announce the punishment are taken from the encounter between God and the Israelites at Sinai (see Exodus 19). In ancient times God told the people to prepare to meet God in what would have been essentially a blessing. Here the reverse is true. The people will meet their God through the terrible disciplines of history.

In verse 13 Amos concludes this oracle with the first of three short segments of hymns. As in 5:8-9 and 9:5-6, each contains the affirmation of God's name using the formula, *The* LORD *is his name.*

§ § § § § § §

The Message of Amos 3–4

Amos begins this section by unequivocally stating election's peril as well as its promise. Popular religion is concerned mainly with public displays of piety and worship. Amos's argument is that Israel's worship is just as evil as pagan rituals. Each chases after superstition. Each imagines God primarily concerned with right "religious" behavior. Amos differs. Amos holds that God wants individuals and nations who will heed divine discipline and return to God's intentions. Amos's contention is that the ultimate end of any culture has to do with the moral questions raised by and implied by God's purposes.

§ Election as God's chosen carries with it the burden of higher responsibility.

§ God is offended by hollow or insincere worship.

§ God has been patient and long-suffering in attempting to reach the nations.

§ God's patience has a limit.

§ Courageous challenging of popular preconceptions will be done through individuals or, at best, minorities.

§ The prophetic stance is always a minority position.

§ Historical events are not necessarily at random.

§ To an extent we do control our futures by making appropriate moral decisions.

§ God reveals God's purposes to human beings.

§ § § § § § §

Amos 5–6

Introduction to These Chapters

National religion offered only a false security of ritual and ceremony. Amos strips away all the pretense of the cultic religion. Even the long-yearned-for Day of the Lord, which had traditionally been a hope for glorious vindication of Israel, will yield darkness and gloom. Violation of God's intention evokes a terrible and final end.

At this juncture we should remember that Amos, though third in the canonical arrangement of the Twelve, actually prophesied first chronologically. Therefore, theological insights and assertions will differ from prophets who wrote following him in chronological time. In Hosea for instance, we have already seen God's anguish as God looks upon the same nation with a desperate hope that Israel will return. In one sense Amos's theological perspective is almost without mercy. The requirement of God's law is, for Amos, absolute and inescapable. Hosea, in the wake of what sounds like nearly merciless prophecy of Amos, had to wrestle with the questions that Amos leaves unanswered.

Here is an outline of Amos 5 and 6.
 I. Israel's Just Reward for Sin (5:1-27)
   A. The prophet's lament (5:1-3)
   B. God's appeal to Israel (5:4-17)
   C. The Day of the Lord (5:18-20)

D. The noise of ritual (5:21-27)
II. Oracles of an Inevitable Doom (6:1-14)
A. Oracles against the idle rich (6:1-7)
B. An oracle of imminent disaster (6:8-14)

The Prophet's Lament (5:1-3)

Amos does not ignore religious traditions. In this oracle he begins by using the traditional language and form of the lament (David sang a lament upon the deaths of Saul and Jonathan; see 2 Samuel 1:17-27). He does not abandon the older traditions. Instead, he reinterprets them through a radically new use of an ancient tradition. Once again the messenger formula introduces the oracle (recall 3:1; 4:1; see 8:4).

Though the forces of history will be let loose against Israel, Amos does show two moments of compassion for the nation. Here the prophet sings a funeral song over the fallen nation. Later on he intercedes on behalf of the nation (see 7:1-6).

The extent of war's devastation can be lost on no one. The entire military is nearly destroyed. For the remaining tenth of the population an unsure future holds little promise.

God's Appeal to Israel (5:4-17)

Whatever hope Amos harbors is wrapped up in the request by God for the return of Israel (verses 5-6). By implication there may yet be a shred of hope, if only Israel will return by seeking God. Amos's own trust in the peoples' choice seems slim indeed (5:15).

Amos's listeners would have been familiar with the tradition of seeking guidance or direction. Rebekah had asked for insight regarding the struggling twins (see Genesis 25:22). Kings frequently sought direction or an oracle before entering battle (see Jeremiah 21:2). But even in the invitation comes an implicit acknowledgment that the nation will not return to God by seeking God through oracle or prophet. Instead, pilgrims will insist on journeys to the national sanctuaries at Bethel and Gilgal.

Beersheba (in Hebrew *well of the oath*) is named in the tradition of Abraham (see Genesis 21:31-32, where Abraham settles a water dispute with Abimelech). This site was in Judean territory directly adjacent to Israel.

Fire is used to describe the means by which the Lord will execute judgment (see 1:4, 7, 10, 12; 2:2, 5).

Wormwood (NRSV; NIV= *bitterness*) is a plant with a terribly bitter taste (6:12).

Justice and *righteousness* (verse 7) are central tenets in Amos's prophecy. Here and in 6:12 Amos uses justice as part of an indictment. In 5:15, 24 the same term is part of God's larger intention for the land. In Amos's prophecy justice is the only means by which the weaker members of society can expect protection against the power of the wealthy.

The court consisted of wealthy or influential men of the community. They met in one of the city gates to hear complaints brought against fellow citizens. Formal trial proceedings as we understand court process were lacking. Instead, the complaint would be considered and a judgment made. The image evoked by Amos is of innocent yet poor people unable to receive a fair hearing for their complaints. The wealthy would join together, thus silencing the plaintiff.

Amos uses the term *righteousness* to describe the appropriate action taken to defend an innocent individual in the court and thus maintain social relationships. Society itself is jeopardized when justice is perverted and righteousness ignored.

Verses 8-9 are the second of three doxologies. Their placement seems to interrupt the description of travesties of justice (verse 10 could easily continue without the interruption). However, the hymn immediately follows Amos's admonition not to seek God at the sanctuary in Bethel. God cannot be located in a shrine. God is the God of the heavens, of the entire universe. The same God of the stars (see Job 9:9; 38:31) is the God of history. Wars are not mere accidents of national policies. Wars are a part of God's sovereign power. Against the superstition of the ritualists Amos places the authority of God's power.

Court proceedings (verse 10) require accurate and truthful testimony. The Ten Commandments prohibit false witness (Exodus 20:16).

Having made his indictment clear, Amos moves in verse 11 to the statement of judgment. With a rapidly expanding economy and subsequent growth of cities, Israel—people of the earth, agricultural workers—lost power in both the economy and social/political structures. The poorer people would have to rent land from wealthier owners. City-dwelling landlords received income at the expense of the relatively powerless poor. Excessive rents or taxes financed building projects. The rich enjoyed fine homes while poor folk languished in debt.

God intends to reverse the comfort of the wealthy and the lot of the poor. The wealthy will not be allowed to enjoy their luxury. All the while they amassed their fortunes and built their homes, the rich considered themselves to be beyond the scope of God's vision or concern. Amos disintegrates that blithe confidence by contending that those who took land will themselves have their land taken.

The prophet states in verse 12 that God has seen and knows what the rich have done. The wealthy have conspired against the poor by taking bribes (see Exodus 23:8) and by rejecting the entreaties of the poor (see Exodus 23:6; Isaiah 10:2; Malachi 3:5).

Verse 13 sounds like an inclusion from the wisdom tradition. Its counsel is well-heeded. In a time when the courts themselves are corrupt, one is well advised to measure one's words and be silent. When argument with others yields little more than intensified conspiracy, one needs to wait upon the justice of God.

In verses 14-15 Amos parodies the worship litanies of popular religion. The pairings—seek good, not evil; hate evil, love good—are similar to arrangements of proverbs (for example: Proverbs 12:1; 13:24; see also Psalm 34:14).

The people intone their litany but do not substantiate it with appropriate behavior. Doubtless the original hearers did not comprehend Amos's parody of their worship. Doing religion too frequently is reserved for activities within the structures, both physical and institutional, of organized religion. *Not everyone who says to me "Lord, Lord" will enter the kingdom of heaven* (Matthew 7:21). Amos's theology is that God may be present only when people authentically seek to do the will of God through behavior consistent with the character and intention of God (see Micah 6:6-8). Amos links the litany with social relationships.

Amos does not go on to say that appropriate moral behavior obligates God to bless Israel. God is still free to choose whom God will bless. If civic or popular religion is the most difficult of entanglements to sort out, surely the notion that pious behavior or "church going" in some sense obligates God is a close second. A works-righteousness attitude is not restricted to Protestantism or Pharisaism. The problem is a universally human one. Amos dares to state the utter freedom of God to choose.

The remnant of Joseph may refer to survivors of Tiglath-pileser's invasion and subsequent deportation of Gilead and Galilee in 734 B.C.

The oracle continues in verses 16-17 with the Lord speaking through the image of a funeral (see Jeremiah 9:17-22; Micah 2:4). The entire city will echo with grief-stricken lament. The oppressed farmers whose moaning had been ignored by the wealthy will themselves be the mourners at the wealthy ones' funerals.

The exact nature of how God will execute judgment is not indicated. But the judgment will be God's nonetheless.

The Day of the Lord (5:18-20)

The notion that there will come a day when God will vindicate Israel against all of her enemies had no doubt been in circulation for quite some time. All popular hopes seek their results in this day. The term occurs in many other writings: Isaiah 2:12; 13:6, 9; 22:5; 34:8; Jeremiah 46:10; Ezekiel 7:10; 13:5; 30:3; Joel 1:15; 2:1; Obadiah 15; Zephaniah 1:7, 14-18; Zechariah 14:1. Since Amos is the first writing prophet, the term occurs here in writing for the first time.

As in other recitations of popular religious thinking (salvation history, 2:9-11, and election, 3:2), Amos confronts Israel with startling reverses to popular expectations. The utter confidence of the people evokes a woe oracle. The images of the Day allude to darkness and gloom (see Isaiah 13:10; Ezekiel 30:3; Joel 2:1-2; Zephaniah 1:15-16). The images Amos uses from nature would have been quite familiar to the listeners. They may well have seen a terrified man flee to his home only to find in it another threat to life.

The Noise of Ritual (5:21-27)

Earlier Amos characterized the people as loving ritual and ceremony (4:5). Here all subtlety is placed aside. Amos places the habits of worship against the moral expectations in social systems. Amos speaks the harsh word of the Lord against the worship of Israel. Could any word have been more startling and alarming? With some imagination we might see a wide-eyed and shocked people.

The oracle attacks all of the major elements in Israel's worship. Three major feasts marked the liturgical year (see Exodus 23:14-17; 34:18-24): Unleavened

Bread/Passover, Feast of Weeks, and the Festival of the Harvest/Succoth. Amos also condemns offerings and sacrifices, as well as praises and songs. With a single utterance the entire worship life of Israel is condemned.

The Lord's condemnation is not an arbitrary judgment that takes its cue from poorly performed worship. The quality of worship takes its cue from the moral substance of the worshiper's life. God's judgment comes when the people hide behind their religion. The people have confused concentrating on the forms of ritual and worship for the critical work of justice and righteousness demanded by God for the ordering of society. The people have been as fickle in their moral lives as a stream bed in the wilderness. In rainy seasons wadis fill to a gushing overflow. In dry seasons they are nothing more than dried up riverbeds worthless to a parched land. God demands justice and righteousness that flow constantly.

Verse 24 can well be considered the heart of Amos's preaching. *But let justice roll down like waters, and righteousness like an everflowing stream* (NRSV).

In verses 25-27 Amos returns to the motif of God's action in history. Evidently the priests of the sanctuaries had ceased preaching about the saving acts of God in Israel's past. Priests' work focused primarily on the performance of the worshiper through ritual. Amos alludes to a time when Israel's worship was pristine, in the wilderness, before the development of cultic worship centers and rituals. Other prophets also allude to the wilderness (Jeremiah 2:1-2; Hosea 2:14-15).

Sakkuth and *Kaiwan* (NRSV) may be derivations of words meaning *tabernacles* and *pedestal* (NIV). However, Amos's use of the terms suggests they are names of or allusions to Assyrian gods.

The reference to the wilderness in verse 27 evokes the memory of God's saving act. The same God will act in judgment against the people of God's own election. The chosen people will be separated from the chosen land.

Oracles Against the Idle Rich (6:1-7)

Amos begins a new set of oracles against the idle rich with a woe oracle. The oracle consists of: (1) indictments of arrogant self-confidence of the wealthy (verses 1-3) and of luxury (verse 4), (2) disregard for covenant brothers and sisters (verses 5-6), and (3) an announcement of punishment (verse 7).

Zion is another name for the royal city of Jerusalem. Samaria was a fortress city purchased and built by Omri (see 1 Kings 16:23-24).

Amos calls attention to the major cities *Hamath* (see 6:14) and *Calneh* that had been overwhelmed by Assyrian power.

The evil day is another term for the Day of the Lord. The oracle characterizes commercial cities arrogantly unaware of their fate.

The rich eat only the finest foods, idly listen to music, imbibe on drink, but wreak moral havoc on their brothers and sisters, the poor.

At the head of the long lines of refugees will be the once-proud and overindulged wealthy (verse 7). Jesus employs this terrible insight into history (see Luke 6:24-25).

An Oracle of Imminent Disaster (6:8-14)

Oracles of imminent disaster are addressed to the prideful nation. The intensity of God's conviction is expressed through the Lord invoking the Lord's own name. Amos uses this form in two other instances (4:2 and 8:7).

The pride of Jacob refers to the smug self-confidence of Israel's leaders and wealthy class. Israel had turned the once-historical faith into nothing more than a distasteful and self-indulgent pride (see Isaiah 28:1; Hosea 5:5). This pride is more dependent upon fortresses than upon trust in God.

Verses 9-10 may appear as an intrusion. However, they

describe the extent of the disaster that will befall Israel. Traditionally bodies were not burned. Recall that in an earlier oracle (2:1) the Moabites were condemned because they defiled the dead. What Amos does in this short description is to show how even a longstanding tradition will buckle under the onslaught of utter devastation. Amos drives home his point through stark images of unclean houses, family members afraid to search the ruins, and finally a single voice of a survivor who can hardly mention the name of the Lord any longer. Nothing in popular religion equipped survivors for disaster of this magnitude.

Shattering the popular conception of a benevolent God concerned only with the developing wealth of Israel, Amos contends that no less than the Lord caused the catastrophe (verses 11-14).

In verse 12 Amos asks absurd questions while in the same breath mentioning the highest callings of the Lord. In placing the absurdities and highest callings together Amos shows the extent to which Israel has distorted God's intentions.

From Hamath to Arabah points to the extremities of Israel's expansion and resurgence under Jeroboam II (see 2 Kings 14:23-25). God will raise up a nation against Israel. The chapter ends with a threat of doom hanging over the complacent settled faith of the age.

§ § § § § § §

The Message of Amos 5–6

The oracles in this section are all addressed to a people who have forgotten their primary responsibility as the people of God. National resurgence, military successes, remarkable economic growth with attendant luxuries of fine homes and sumptuous living had all dulled the moral senses. What can we learn from these chapters?

§ God wants people to seek God.

§ Seeking God is the way to real life.

§ The prophetic faith sees the Lord at work in all of history.

§ In the Bible the poor are not the problem. Instead, the rich are a problem to the poor.

§ Unless moral obligations to the poor and weak are kept, worship becomes little more than noise and empty ceremony.

§ God is worshiped through caring social relationships as well as hymns and prayers.

§ No sin is as scathingly condemned as the sin of pride.

§ Under sufficient stress of history, popular religion will buckle. When it does, the prophet will inform the nation of a larger God in whose hands lies all of history.

§ § § § § § §

Amos 7

Introduction to This Chapter

Chapter 7 affords a glimpse into the personal life of the prophet. Amos describes visions that have come to him, speaks of an attempted intercession, and then narrates his dramatic confrontation with the royal priest Amaziah.

Among the earliest instructions given to any preacher in introductory homiletics classes is not to preach oneself. Amos does not preach himself. Instead, he speaks of his own personal experience as it reveals the will of God and the authority behind the prophet's work.

Here is an outline of these chapters:
I. Judgment and Visions (7:1-9)
   A. Judgment by locusts (7:1-3)
   B. Judgment by fire (7:4-6)
   C. Vision of the plumb line (7:7-9)
II. Conflict and Confrontation (7:10-17)

Judgment and Visions (7:1-9)

Visions are common in prophetic experience. When Jehoshaphat inquires of the prophet Micaiah, the prophet responds, *I saw all Israel scattered* (1 Kings 22:1-53, especially verse 17). Isaiah's narrative of his conversion includes a vision of the Lord (see Isaiah 6). Jeremiah records visions in his call to prophetic ministry (Jeremiah 1:11-14). For other instances see Ezekiel 1:8-9; Zechariah 1:8. In each instance Amos asserts God's own authority for the vision, *the Sovereign* LORD (NIV; NRSV = LORD *God*) *showed me* (7:1, 4, 7).

Judgment by Locusts (7:1-3)

Locust plagues were not uncommon (see Joel 1:2-7 where Joel works with an actual disaster afflicting the people). This particular swarm's arrival will be at a critical time, just before the last crop of the season. Verse 1 may allude to the government's confiscation of crops for the army.

Perhaps somewhat surprisingly, given the fact that Amos had been prophesying national disaster and exile, the prophet intercedes for the people. Now Amos sees the weakness of the people. They cannot stand the catastrophe of natural disaster if it does come.

Other individuals interceded on behalf of peoples or cities. Some of the intercessors were prophets (Abraham in Genesis 20:7; an unnamed man on behalf of Jeroboam in 1 Kings 13:6; Elisha on behalf of the widow's son in 2 Kings 4:33).

Genesis 18:16-33 relates the dialogue between Abraham and the Lord regarding the fate of Sodom and Gomorrah. In that dialogue Abraham argues the case for the entire population through concern for a few. In Exodus 32:7-14 Moses argues with God about the fate of the stiff-necked Israelites. Numbers 14:11-23 narrates the exchange between Moses and God due to the people's despising God.

The appeal to God is an appeal for mercy. The proud and arrogant nation does not realize its utter vulnerability. Only the prophet and God realize this.

In response to Amos's intercession God *relents*, that is, changes God's own mind.

Two further comments need to be made about Amos's ministry of intercession. God and the prophet know the people better than the people know themselves. The prayers of cultic or popular religion focused on ritual and national interests of security and prosperity. Amos's prayers have to do with the utter dependency of the people on the graces of the eternal. God knows the people's needs better than they do. The second observation is that the people probably were completely unaware of the prophet's ministry on their behalf. The apparently outrageous prophecies offended the people. Presently Amos himself will give moving testimony to the conflict with established royal religion. Few if any could have imagined the prophet praying on their behalf. The devastation was stayed by the decision of God. While speaking oracles of doom, the prophet still prays for his people.

Judgment by Fire (7:4-6)

The image of fire is frequently used as a metaphor for God's judgment (recall 1:4, 7, 10 for instance; also Leviticus 10:2 and Numbers 11:1. One of the most well known instances is the trial by fire narrated in 1 Kings 18).

This vision, like that of the locusts, is of an event that has not yet occurred.

The great deep refers to a sea presumed to be beneath the earth from which all springs and rivers flowed.

The land refers to the land of Israel through which God blessed the people.

Vision of the Plumb Line (7:7-9)

The two previous visions clearly showed destruction as punishment. This vision has symbolic meaning. In this vision Amos sees the Lord (see Isaiah 6:1; Amos 9:1). Whereas Amos comprehended the visions of locusts and fire, the Lord must interpret the vision of the plumb line. Against the absolute measure of God's will and covenant expectations, the people are hopelessly crooked.

The days of pleading and repenting are over for God. In days past God passed by or over Israel. The allusion to the dreadful plague of death that afflicted the first-born of Egypt would not be lost on Israel. Now, however, God will pass through Israel as well.

Isaac is used in verse 9 for the only time as the name for the Northern Kingdom.

High places refers to shrines on hilltops first erected under the authority of Jeroboam I. Major sanctuaries were located in Bethel (see 7:13), the shrine for the southern extremities of Israel, and Dan, in the northern extremity of the kingdom.

God's punishment will be through warfare (*sword*, see 9:1, 4) against the dynasty of Jeroboam as well as the balance of the nation (see 2 Kings 21:13-15). Quite clearly Assyria is the oncoming agent. In fact, precisely this destruction occurred to Jeroboam's son Zechariah (see 2 Kings 15:8-10).

Conflict And Confrontation (7:10-17)

The previous oracle mentioned the sanctuary in Bethel. Using this reference as a linking key, Amos presents the dramatic narrative of his confrontation with Amaziah, the royal priest.

Apparently Amos had been preaching for quite some time. Strong words fell on deaf ears; urgency was lost in the complacency of affluence. Unlike most other prophets who uttered their words at a safe distance from the offending party, Amos travels to the very center of the national/cultic religion in Bethel. What follows is one of the classic confrontations of history—the man of God versus the man of the king. The man with an eternal word confronts the man with an expedient word. In the confrontation of priest against prophet, the one stands with the king behind him, and the other stands with God beside him.

Amaziah is not mentioned anyplace else in the Scriptures. In all likelihood he was the chief priest of the royal sanctuary. Why would the man with royal authority be anxious about a country preacher?

Perhaps Amaziah studied history. The history of Israel contains illustrations of the need for support by prophets.

Ahijah, a prophet from Shiloh, had opposed King Jeroboam (see 1 Kings 11:29–12:24; 15:29; 2 Chronicles 10:15). He had acted out in prophetic fashion the fate of the kingdom if Jeroboam continued his disastrous policies (1 Kings 11:26-40). A prophet could make a difference in who governs. Elijah and other prophets influenced who would govern during the ascendancy of Jeroboam II. The prophet Elisha fomented Jehu's rebellion against King Ahab (see 2 Kings 9:1-14). For all Amaziah could tell, Amos too may have been a revolutionary conspirator. Had he come to the very center of Israel's life in order to stir up revolt?

The drama begins in verse 10 with Amaziah's report to the worried king. Only the single name, *Amos*, is mentioned. Presumably Amos was well known in official circles. Without giving an exact account of Amos's preaching, the spokesman tells the king just enough of a self-serving truth. Jeroboam will not die a violent death; however, much of Amos's preaching is summarized (see 2:13-16; 3:9-15; 4:1-3; 5:1-3, 16-17; 6:7; 9:2-4). Whether or not the land can tolerate this kind of preaching may be a moot question. Amaziah and the government cannot long tolerate it! The scene will be played out again in the New Testament when the people blurt out the condemning characterization of Jesus' preaching, "He sets himself against Caesar" (John 19:12).

Amos had repeatedly attacked the familiar patterns of ritual worship: both Bethel (4:4-5; 5:4-5) and cultic worship as a whole (5:21-24; 9:1). The ruling dynasty of Jeroboam was also threatened with destruction by a yet unnamed enemy. By raising questions in the worshipers' minds Amos diluted the authority of the government and cultic religion. In one sense the royal interests had a great deal to fear from Amos. But it was not an organized campaign.

Amaziah, threatened by Amos's searching, instructs him to leave Bethel. At least Amos does not suffer the anguish of punishment and terror when he challenges Amaziah. Jeremiah will in his own ministry go through persecution due to his prophetic word (see Jeremiah 20:2). Organized religion had long since stopped asking the difficult questions that history itself forces. Amaziah's authority is the royal power of rule and position. The king's sanctuary is more important than God to this small-minded man! Amaziah attempted to shut the prophet down by employing all of the official authorities he could muster. Vested interest and power cannot long tolerate probing questions.

Amaziah indicates a misunderstanding of what Amos's responsibility really is. Perhaps as a reflection of how Amaziah understands his own religious vocation, he understands only that the preacher is making a living. Preaching of Amaziah's sort can be done anywhere. Therefore, he instructs Amos to leave Bethel.

Amos's response to the admonition in verse 14 gives ample illustration of the prophet's authority. To begin with, the scene must have been one of incredulity on Amaziah's part. How many would-be preachers had been chased from the sanctuary or environs after the invocation of government authority? But Amos refuses. His authority is the authority of the higher calling. In the book of Acts, Peter and John respond to a similar challenge, *We cannot keep from speaking about what we have seen and heard* (Acts 4:19-20).

Amos cites no qualifications from his own life for the work of prophecy. In fact, Amos denies any relationship with prophets or the prophetic tradition. Amos's summons to prophetic ministry came without warning and without his request.

Amos has been instructed by God to speak to Israel. To

Amos the case is quite clear. Amaziah's instructions are not against Amos but against the very God of Israel! The conflict is not primarily between two men of different character. The conflict, as Amos understands it, is between the God of Israel and the people of Israel, whether they are ordinary citizens or government officials.

One of the ironies of history is that the attempt by court officials at silencing the prophet only created another means by which God would continue speaking to the nation. Since Amos is forbidden to speak, he commits his work to writing. Hence, literary or writing prophets have their beginning.

Because Amaziah has cast his lot with the established institutions and interests of government, he too will undergo the exact fate predicted for the dynasty (verse 17). The oracle is very unusual since it is directed towards the individual. Destruction and exile loom large in Amaziah's future. The form of the oracle is quite common, with the customary elements of a required hearing, indictment, the messenger formula, and finally the punishment.

One of the strongest temptations when studying the Bible is to see in it heroic characters, many of whom are larger than life. But the Bible does not understand itself in the same way. The Bible presents characters, some of whom have been apprehended by God to do a courageous act on God's behalf. The triumph at Bethel is not primarily a triumph of Amos's character. The victory is one of God's authority in the life of an individual or a nation. The highest understanding of religion perceives this and cherishes it.

§ § § § § § §

The Message of Amos 7

The seventh chapter of Amos contains a variety of material: oracles, vision reports, and the dramatic narrative of the confrontation with Amaziah. God will use all these means to make God's will known to Israel. God may even use apparently unqualified individuals to carry God's word to the hearts of people. What else can we learn from the chapter?

§ God can use nature to reach the hearts of people.
§ Intercessory prayer may affect a person's life.
§ A true prophet cares for the people.
§ The Bible never understands God in the abstract. In the Bible, God is a being with moral purpose and power.
§ God has countless forms of power that can be used to effect faithful response to God's will.
§ Against God's measure all humanity falls short.
§ God will lift up a prophet in times of national need.
§ The prophet's authority rests not in personal character but instead in God's will and instruction.

§ § § § § § §

Amos 8–9

Introduction to These Chapters

Following the confrontation in Bethel, Amos's
prophecy continues with visions of increasing
immediacy. The end of Israel is not far off now. The
question raised in Amos's thinking is, What will survive?
Institutions, government, rituals, and customs may be
obliterated by an enemy. What will survive and endure?
For Amos the heart of faith will survive: trust in the
ultimate power of God, true religion that has moral
sensitivity and social obligation as its motives. Amos
makes sense of the impending disaster by interpreting it
as a means of discipline and not merely an utter doom.

Here is an outline of Amos 8–9.
  I. A Vision and an Indictment (8:1-14)
    A. The basket of summer fruit (8:1-3)
    B. An oracle of indictment (8:4-14)
 II. The Finality of Israel's Doom (9:1-10)
    A. Vision of the Lord (9:1-4)
    B. A doxology (9:5-6)
    C. God's freedom (9:7-10)
III. A Promise of Restoration (9:11-15)

The Basket of Summer Fruit (8:1-3)

As with the vision of the plumb line, this vision is a
symbolic one. Amos employs a play on words which is
lost to us in English translations. In Hebrew the word for
fruit is *qayits*. The word for *end* (NRSV; NIV = *the time is*

ripe) is *qets*. A similar play on words occurs in Jeremiah's vision of the almond branch. There the similar sounding words are *almond* (in Hebrew *shaqed*) and *watching* (in Hebrew *shoqed*) (see Jeremiah 1:11-12). On first hearing the oracle begins with what appears to be hope: harvest. However, the oracle quickly turns to a forecast of doom: end.

Songs will turn to wailings in that day, that is, the Day of the Lord. References to the Temple and *every place* imply that judgment begins with the institutions of national or cultic/popular religion. No facile hope for the sanctity of God's own house will suffice.

An Oracle of Indictment (8:4-14)

The third major section of Amos's prophecy begins here in verse 4.

Amos sees the sacred sabbath threatened with the same greed that had affected the social and court orderings. The enemies of the sabbath are the enemies of the poor and oppressed.

Amos begins by demanding the attention of wrongdoers. In a sarcastic tone Amos parodies the merchants' own statements. Recall that earlier Amos had parodied the litanies of worship (4:4-5).

Amos restated the theme of treatment of the poor (see 2:6; 4:1; 5:12). The sad plight of the poor is that they continue descending into greater debt and poverty while the rich increase their wealth and power.

In verse 5 Amos pictures merchants intoning liturgy while all the while impatiently waiting for worship to conclude so they can continue their amassing of wealth.

New moon refers to the first day of the lunar month (see 2 Kings 4:23; Isaiah 1:13-14; Hosea 2:11). The observance of this day was added to the observance of the sabbath (See Exodus 23:12).

An *ephah* (NRSV; NIV = *measure*) is a unit of dry

measure equaling one tenth of a homer or approximately two-thirds of bushel.

False balances (NRSV; NIV = *dishonest scales*) are the bane of commercial and economic relationships. Apparently merchants would frequently use a set of weights for wealthy friends different from that used for poor customers. Early in Israel's tradition the use of false weights was specifically forbidden (see Leviticus 19:35; Deuteronomy 25:13-16). Wisdom literature also speaks against the practice (Proverbs 20:10). Micah also condemns false weights (see Micah 6:10).

The plight of the poor has reached such depths that they must subsist on the chaff and trash remaining after the threshing. Worse yet, the merchants see only another means by which to increase wealth. The poor have been dehumanized into little more than ciphers in an economic system.

God takes an oath in which God sides with the poor. Never will God forget the mean-spirited merchants.

In verse 8 Amos uses a piece from a hymn to describe the consequences of God's outrage. The metaphors underscore the authority and power of the never-forgetting God.

The Lord speaks in verses 9-10. Amos's voice has been a minority voice. The great majority of people and prophets alike have chanted a confident litany of God's salvation for Israel. Now God challenges the popularly-held assumption with the dreadful announcement of a grim and darkened midday. Eclipses did occur during the years 803 and 763 B.C. The time of this particular event is deliberately left ambiguous. The saying implies, *There will come a time* (see 2:16).

Graphic scenes of anguish and mourning give personal dimension to the disaster. As the hope of life depends upon the survival of the only son, so the future is grim and hopeless with the death of the son. Deep within the soul of Israel is the story which encapsulates the hope of a future. To Abraham and Isaac an only son meant hope for a continued people. Abraham too had to endure the anguished possibility of his son's death. Doubtless Amos's listeners would recall the dramatic events in the story of the binding of Isaac (see Genesis 22). In the ancient story, however, God intervenes. The sacrifice does not occur. For the Israel in which Amos prophesied, God will take no such action. Indeed, God will be responsible for the disaster.

Following earthquake and eclipse God will work through a unique kind of famine. The oracle in verses 11-14 opens with God's announcement of what will take place.

Comfortable patterns and customs of life will come unglued. Catastrophe has mounted on catastrophe. People are desperate now to have someone make sense of what appears to be chaos. Historically people sought interpretation through the prophet (see 1 Samuel 28:6; 1 Kings 22:5-6) or in a sanctuary through sacrifice (recall Hosea 5:6). Amos himself had summoned the people to seek God in order to live. But the time for that sincere seeking has passed.

The people will search everywhere within the bounds of their imaginations and geography in vain for any authentic word from God. Their cry will be the cry of absence. Their God has abandoned them. Amos sees people thirsting for an authentic word of the Lord. Their institutions have failed them, their enthusiastic worship has proven to be bankrupt, their popular theology has proven barren. What can possibly survive? Amos does not quickly step in to offer a hope. Indeed, amidst helplessness the argument for disaster continues. No segment of society will escape the debilitating anxiety and desperation. Even the strongest will weaken and fail.

Ashimah is the goddess of Hamath.

The statements contend that from the farthest reaches

north (Dan) to the south (Beersheba), all will be engulfed in the disaster.

Vision of the Lord (9:1-4)

This vision constitutes the fifth vision (see also 7:1-9; 8:1-3), and is by far the most devastating.

I saw the LORD summarizes the prophet's authority. The vision comes to Amos in the Temple (see Isaiah 6:1-8). Traditionally a revelation in the Temple would be one assuring people that God had heard prayers or received offerings. Unlike traditional assurances of blessing, this vision is of God as enemy. God's patience with cultic religion and all of its institutions has come to an end.

Capitals (NRSV; NIV = *tops*) refers to the central support pillar of the sanctuary (see Zephaniah 2:14). *Thresholds* are stones into which door posts were set (see Isaiah 6:4). The destruction evokes the memory of Samson's efforts in the temple of the Philistines (see Judges 16:28-30). Any survivors will perish at the edge of the sword. There will be no escape for anyone.

The description of frantic escape efforts in verses 2-4 sounds very much like Psalm 139. However, in the psalm the speaker cannot escape the gracious presence of God. In this utterance the individual cannot escape the grim death brought by God. Even exile will not be enough to save the people.

God has taken two different means by which to inflict punishment. One has been a terrifying absence from the people. The other is a terrible vengeance wreaked on them. God has changed blessing into curse.

Sheol (NRSV; NIV = *the grave*) is the place of the dead (see Job 10:19-22; Isaiah 14:11, 15).

A Doxology (9:5-6)

Verses 5-6 are the third hymn segment in Amos's prophecy (recall 4:13; 5:8-9). In earlier segments the name for God is *the* LORD, *the God of hosts.* Here the term used is *the Lord, GOD of hosts* (NRSV; NIV = *The Lord, the LORD Almighty*). Scholars suggest that since the names used are different, this fragment may have been included at a later time by an editor.

This section follows a dire threat of severe punishment. Perhaps some people questioned the prophet. How can all of this come to pass? What is the power behind it all? To this kind of question comes the affirmation of God's creative power. Amos echoes liturgical affirmations of God's creation. God speaks and the earth melts (see Psalm 46:6). God touches the mountains and they smoke (see Psalm 104:32).

God's Freedom (9:7-10)

Throughout Amos's work the pride of Israel has been especially targeted. Popular religion emphasized the chosenness of Israel and ignored the moral obligations of commerce, social relationships, and justice. Again and again Amos parodied liturgical forms in order to break the bubble of prematurely confident complacency.

Amos has been hinting at a universal God ever since the opening phrase of the opening oracle in his entire prophecy. The nations adjacent to Israel had been included in God's judgment for violating ethics of basic human dignity in time of war. The seed had been planted for what Amos will now contend about God, Israel, and the history of all nations.

God speaks here of the experience of Israel among the family of nations. Amos claims that God has always been at work in all history. This claim would no doubt stir either shock or resentment since much of Israel's history had been a rehearsal of God's unique calling, blessing, and salvation for Israel. The people had grown accustomed to priding themselves that they had been known in a unique way by God (recall 3:2).

In verse 7 Amos mentions the central saving act by God, the salvation from bondage in Egypt. However, the act is placed within a much larger and more common context of history. Throughout history there have been migrations of peoples. God has been at work in those massive migrations just as much as with the specific events surrounding the Exodus from Egypt.

By making this broad assertion, Amos has stripped away any and all of Israel's claims of exclusivity. This short verse obviates exclusive claim, through correct theology, of any hope of preferential treatment during the Day of the Lord, and false security of expanding economic growth during the prosperous years. All of Israel's pride evaporates under the heat of a universal God.

Moreover, Amos emphasizes God's freedom. At the root of ritual or ceremony is the subtle notion that a well-done ceremony in some sense pleases God and obligates God to act benevolently towards the worshiper. Being able to say a correct theology, to affirm an assumed orthodoxy, is another way in which God is pleased. When God is pleased by the action or attitude of an individual or nation, then God is required to act benevolently.

Amos establishes the absolute sovereignty and freedom of God to do as God chooses with whom God chooses to act. For all of its pride, Israel is but another nation in the family of nations. For all of its pride, the nation falls under the same judgment as nations guilty of crass and gross crimes against humanity. God's freedom always exceeds our history. The issue of God's existence depending upon the successful history of the nation is not restricted to ancient peoples struggling to make sense of military-political disasters. Modern nations too see their history in some sense obligating God's benevolent action and blessing.

Caphtor refers to Crete and the Philistines.

Kir means the Mesopotamians or Arameans.

Parallel to God's absolute freedom to choose is God's

moral claim on all people (see verse 8). A universal God at work through all history is also the source for universal ethics. Israel will suffer punishment for its sin as others suffer through history for their sins.

The second part of verse 8 speaks of a surviving remnant from the house of Jacob. Up to this point Amos has given no indication of any hope for escape. In previous oracles he has predicted that if any survivors did escape, they would subsequently be executed even in exile. Scholars conclude that this section was probably added at a later time, perhaps by a writer from the southern kingdom of Judah.

Even now, some still claim that no harm will come to them or to their beloved nation (verse 10). To them a special word is given. Amos turns the words of the self-serving back on them (recall 2:12; 4:1; 5:14; 6:13; 7:16; 8:5, 14). The metaphor of a *sieve* used during the threshing of grain suggests just how thoroughly history will work upon Israel.

A Promise of Restoration (9:11-15)

The final section of Amos appears to be from a different hand. These last five verses make the promise of a restored kingdom without any reference to the moral character of the people or God's expectation. Therefore, many scholars conclude that the verses are an addition by a later editor of Amos's work.

The oracle begins with allusion to the Day of the Lord. However, this usage is quite different from previous usages. This day will be a benevolent one of salvation.

Booth (NRSV; NIV = *tent*) could have many meanings. Crudely erected booths protected soldiers, protected water holes, and afforded travelers protection on the way to feasts and festivals. They were also erected as major elements of the festival of Booths/Tabernacles (see Leviticus 23:39-43). The image here is one of protection

HOSEA THROUGH JONAH

and preservation. In this hope is the latent desire to retrieve the old days when things were much better.

The mention of Edom suggests that the later editor shares with Amos the hope of a universal God. Any nationalistic editor or writer with a memory of the historic animosity might easily be excused from including Edom in God's saving grace. Edom had for generations been a particularly evil name. During the last days of Jerusalem in 587 B.C., as the city lay prostrate at the feet of the invader, Edomites joined in the pillage and plunder. Animosity toward the cousin nation that would take advantage of the disaster finds expression in Obadiah (also Lamentations 4:21-22 and Psalm 137).

Verses 11 and 12 are used in the New Testament period by James during the critical Jerusalem Conference (see Acts 15:16-17).

The additional material continues in verses 13-15 with a promise of an idyllic time of fertility and security. As dispirited refugees contemplate scorched earth, as exiles remember only blackened stone, as farmers remember devastating famine, this oracle lifts their eyes to a brighter future. God will once again bless the land and the people.

God can change the fortunes of people for ill or for good; now God will change the fortunes of the people for good (see Deuteronomy 30:3; Job 42:10; Psalm 126:1-6). The once-embattled people will again enjoy the fruits of their labors.

The prophecy ends in verse 15 with the prediction of a permanence for the people. Jeremiah had been summoned to pluck up and to plant. Here the promise is of a deep rooting so that fortunes will not again be reversed. Amos had repeatedly offered a slim hope of grace if the people could only repent. The promise in the concluding verses is an unconditional promise not dependent upon the actions of the people.

§ § § § § § §

The Message of Amos 8–9

Over and over again Amos strained to have people understand the moral obligation that rests heavily on God's people. But just as frequently and with equal verve the people rejected the prophet's pleading. The prophet reaches deeply into history and creation in order to re-present a God capable of working through all history, not just Israel's history, and through all creation, not merely in the creative acts for Israel. In his seeking, Amos discerns a freedom that startles us with its implications.

What can we learn about the nature and character of God from these chapters?

§ God's judgments may be closer than people think.

§ The prophetic urgency for repentance is ridiculed only at individual and national peril.

§ God is the God of all history, not just for Israel or any other nation that desires to see itself as chosen.

§ Our words of pride may come back to haunt us.

§ Worship is of little value if we are preoccupied with how we can pervert justice and amass more fortune.

§ When God wreaks judgment no one can escape the presence of God.

§ God's sovereignty is absolute; God cannot be obligated by anything that individuals or nations do or say.

§ Ultimately God yearns to bless individuals and nations.

§ Even the most evil of nations may be included in the ultimate grace of God.

§ § § § § § §

Introduction to Obadiah

The prophecy of Obadiah consists of merely twenty-one verses, making it the shortest book in the Old Testament. The work focuses on the historic enemy Edom, and its reprehensible attitude and behavior during the final collapse of Jerusalem.

The name *Obadiah* means *servant of the Lord*. The name is not unique, in that another twelve individuals share it in the Old Testament (see 1 Kings 18:3; 1 Chronicles 3:21; Ezra 8:9; Nehemiah 10:5). Other than Obadiah's name we know nothing specific about him. Unlike other prophets, he lists no dates of his work, no family identity, no occupation, and no home territory.

Historical Circumstances

What can we deduce from Obadiah's work? He speaks of the dreadful events that occurred when Jerusalem finally fell to the Babylonians in 587 B.C. Obadiah makes many references to other prophetic works, especially Jeremiah 49:7-22. One possibility is that the work is in part a collection of material assembled from various extant prophetic works that Obadiah re-presented and reinterpreted to his people. Since the work does focus on a single theme of God's justice and judgment, scholars hold that it is the work of one writer who uses other material. While we cannot date Obadiah to one year, it appears to have been written while the prophet and his people languished in exile.

The prophet's attitude parallels that of another exile,

who wrote Psalm 137. The last three verses of Psalm 137 are rarely read in Christian worship services. The soul-deep anger, the graphic expression of hate, a yearned-for day when an enemy will have to pay for what was done to innocent people are simply too strong for most of us. But shallow piety and sentimentality were not an option for the pained exiles. The memories ran too deep. We have a record of how deeply the people of God yearned for a day of vindication. The Bible does not blink or flinch at even the harshest of human realities.

The Edomites

The Edomites were descendants of Esau (see Genesis 25:30; 36:1). Like their ancestor, they had little regard for spiritual values. They are never referred to for their gods. They seem to have been a nation with little or no conscience or ideals. Certainly their reprehensible behavior upon the collapse of their neighbor gives stark evidence of a dearth of human decency. In effect, the Edomites displayed an opposite temper from that of the people of Israel, just as Esau had displayed callous shallowness when he sold his birthright for a meal of pottage (see Genesis 25:29-34).

Whatever virtue the Edomites had stemmed from their commercial interests. The nation found itself located at the intersection of many trade routes. From this interest the Edomites developed a shrewd business sense and a wisdom about worldly things (verse 8). Jeremiah also refers to this peculiar wisdom, *Is there no longer wisdom in Teman? Has counsel perished from the prudent? Has their wisdom vanished?* (see Jeremiah 49:7).

Topographically Edom found itself in the relatively secure mountainous (and therefore inaccessible) region to the southeast of the Dead Sea. Thus the Edomites enjoyed a relatively secure existence without the international disruptions endured by their northern neighbors. However, the shadow side of this relative calm is that Edom developed an attitude of callous disregard for others as well as a self-sufficiency that rejected the notion of God's protection and providence.

The Message of Obadiah

Since the book concentrates on the long-hated Edomites' doom, why is it included in the Bible? It seems to have small spiritual insight or message. It speaks not a word about sin, mercy, or righteousness. Like the author of Psalm 137, Obadiah believed passionately in the higher values and aspirations of life and of the nation. He had seen all that he held highest and dearest thoroughly demolished, while a hated enemy only scoffed and then participated in the looting and killing. Obadiah went into exile with his blood boiling, remembering the taunts of the conquerors. But then the scoffing words would not be the last words.

The higher values of life are God's, and they cannot be destroyed. Not only will God have the last word against Edom, but God will have the last word in the lives of all nations. On Obadiah's experience, or one very much like it, another psalmist reflected, *Those who go out weeping, bearing the seed for sowing, shall come home with shouts of joy* (Psalm 126:6).

Obadiah 1-21

Introduction to These Chapters

The book of Obadiah contains a series of short oracles concerning the fate of the Edomite nation. Here is an outline of Obadiah.

   I. Title and Introduction (verse 1)
  II. Destruction of Edom (verses 2-14)
     A. A warning (verses 2-4)
     B. Complete destruction (verses 5-9)
     C. Reason for judgment (verses 10-14)
 III. The Day of the Lord (verses 15-21)
     A. The Day of the Lord (verses 15-16)
     B. A role for survivors (verses 17-18)
     C. Promise of Israel's restoration (verses 19-21)

Title and Introduction (verse 1)

The name *Obadiah* means *one who serves the Lord*. The prophecy, like others, is described as a vision (see Nahum 1:1). Obadiah has an inspired insight into the purposes of God at a time when others around the prophet can see only death, destruction, and a mocking enemy. The prophet takes his own impulses of hatred, which he shares with others, and channels them into a creative and life-giving prophecy. He can see the work of God through history. Edom and all nations will eventually be judged. Hatred itself is not enough to live a life on. The prophet and his people need hope.

The prophecy begins with the messenger formula, *This*

is what the Sovereign L<small>ORD</small> *says* (NIV; NRSV = *Thus says the* L<small>ORD</small>), which establishes the authority of the work. The prophet will need no further authority. The oracles are directed at a specific people: the Edomites. Other prophets singled out a people for God's punishment (see Micah 2:3). The specific wrong for which the Edomites will be held accountable is the collaboration with the enemy during the final collapse of Jerusalem in 587 B.C.

Obadiah's use of *we* implies a Judean audience.

The prophet's insight begins with seeing God using people (see Isaiah 45:1; Jeremiah 43:10), even though those people would never realize that they had been used by God (see Isaiah 10:5-7; Micah 4:12).

Edom is the territory to the southeast of Judah/Palestine.

A Warning (verses 2-4)

Obadiah utters his oracle against Edom while among his own people. Generally prophets did not actually travel to the foreign audience. An exception to this rule is Amos, who traveled to the sanctuary at Bethel. The story of Jonah also pictures the prophet traveling to Nineveh. Obadiah, on the other hand, speaks to his own people in order to help them understand that the events that will swallow Edom are events directed by the God of Israel/Judah. The events are not merely accidents of history.

The word for *rock* is *sela*. Sela is also the name of the Edomite capital city. The Edomite attitude is a smug confidence that the rugged terrain insures its impregnability. But God will not forever tolerate national pride. The offending nation can never escape the justice of God.

The Edomites cannot imagine defeat. Indeed, they seem to imagine themselves above the events of history. No one can bring them down. To the defeated and exiled people of Judah, certainly the Edomite arrogance seems well-founded. Edom is, for the moment, quite powerful and comfortable. Obadiah declares that no less than the eternal God vows to topple the arrogant and the proud. God's own word seals the judgment (see also Amos 1:3).

Complete Destruction (verses 5-9)

The previous oracle announced the punishment. This oracle describes the extent of the punishment. Obadiah begins with a common illustration from life. A thief will take only what can be carried or what is of some value. Another illustration gives further illumination. Laborers in the field would leave something behind after the harvest (recall Ruth's gleanings in the field). Obadiah uses parallel images to show how complete the destruction of Edom will be. Nothing of Edom will survive God's punishment.

Esau alludes to the name of the ancestor (see Genesis 36:1, 8, 19).

Obadiah continues in verse 7 with the theme of Edom's future weakness. The Edomites cannot expect any help from any of their allies. The very people whom the Edomites have considered friends will themselves drive the Edomites to face the conquerors alone. Obadiah shows how the actions that Edom has taken will be turned back against the Edomites (see verse 14). Hospitality is a special concern in the Old Testament, especially in the narratives of the patriarchs. In Genesis 18:1-8 Abraham entertains three angels by the oak of Mamre. In Genesis 19:1-11 sojourners are protected by Lot in the city of Sodom. Recall the horror of the events in Gibeah, where the unnamed concubine was brutalized and killed (see also Psalm 41:9).

On *that day* Edom will lose both warriors and its wise men (see Zephaniah 1:9, 10; 3:16; Haggai 2:23).

Mount Esau (see also verses 19 and 21) indicates the mountainous terrain of the Edomite territory.

Soldiers will be thoroughly demoralized (see Exodus 23:27; Deuteronomy 7:23; Joshua 10:10).

In the book of Job, Teman is the home of Eliphaz. This verse refers to the tradition of wisdom associated with the Edomites.

In verses 2 through 9, Obadiah combines the forces of human action and divine purpose. His theological insight is that God will use history to work out moral judgments on nations. Edom may never recognize God's work. Perhaps the forces themselves will never acknowledge the fact that they have been used by God. To the eye of faith, however, all the invaders (thieves, harvesters, and foreign armies) are no less than instruments of the eternal God. Against the purpose of God, Edom's apparent power of wisdom, impregnability, and clever alliances are utterly useless.

Reason for Judgment (verses 10-14)

Following the graphic imagery of destruction, Obadiah tells what Edom's crime is that evokes such devastation.

Jacob was the brother of Esau (Genesis 25–29), and the father of the Israelites (see Genesis 49:2; Isaiah 43:1). The family relationship is a very special one. The violation of family is especially evil. Edom has been willing to break even this most basic of human relationships.

In verse 11 the scene shifts from a general description to a specific series of events. When the Babylonians finally breached the walls of Jerusalem, the entire city lay at the feet of the invader. Worse than simply watching without doing anything to help, the Edomites behaved like the conquerors themselves.

In three stanzas Obadiah lists eight indictments against Edom for its violation of kinship. Each of the stanzas concludes with synonyms for the catastrophe: *misfortune, destruction* (NIV; NRSV = *ruin*), *distress* (NRSV; NIV = *trouble*), *calamity*, and *disaster*.

The Edomites looted along with the enemy (recall

Psalm 137:7-9). Here in verse 13, Obadiah uses the phrase *my people* to show his own solidarity with the victims of the crime. Hatred has blinded the Edomites. They showed no such compassion. Worse yet, the Edomites rejoiced at the disaster that engulfed their neighbors. Other prophets express outrage at such coarse disregard (see Isaiah 34:5-7; 63:1-6; Lamentations 4:21; Ezekiel 25:12-14; Malachi 1:2-5).

Evidently the Edomites positioned themselves at strategic locations to intercept fleeing refugees. The terrified survivors of the slaughter were then summarily turned over to the conquerors.

Edomites relished inflicting needless pain and suffering. Few instances in history can match the human anguish of a kindred nation turning innocent survivors over to a conquering people. However, the prophet sees that the victors are living on borrowed time. Inevitably the victors of today will themselves become victims and will be swept away. Through it all, the memory of innocent people being turned over as victims remains imbedded in the historical memory of Israel.

History appeared to have stripped Israel and Judah of their God. Now Obadiah recovers God for Israel through history.

The Day of the Lord (verses 15-16)

A time will come when God will make right the many wrongs perpetrated against God's intentions. Israel clung to this promise as a means of retaining both faith and sanity when despair and insanity threatened. Popular belief held that the people of God will share in the future victory. Not all prophets held to this belief (see Amos 3:2; 5:18-20). For Obadiah the disaster of the fall of Jerusalem is not the end of God's hope. Those events set God's retributive justice in motion. Many nations had collaborated in the attack, and many nations will feel the wrath of God's judgment.

Drinking the cup of God's wrath expresses God's judgment (see Psalm 75:8). The image of the cup is familiar to Christians from Mark 10:38 and 14:36. All of Israel's tormentors will have to drink from the detestable cup. The nations will be as helpless against God's wrath as a drunken person is against the force of gravity.

A Role for Survivors (verses 17–18)

For generations, Jerusalem was held to be sacrosanct and inviolable. Popular belief was that God would never allow the sacred city to fall. But it did fall. Obadiah recovers the old traditions by contending that, though some of Jerusalem's population will survive, none of the invaders will survive. Even though Israel has suffered God's judgment, Israel is still promised victory through a purified remnant. The theme of the remnant is resumed in verse 21.

Under the leadership of King David, Israel experienced her most glorious expanse of power and territory. During the reign of Jeroboam II, the northern kingdom of Israel experienced a resurgence to its former borders. The memory of those historic eras of grandeur and power haunted Judah. Would the nation ever again achieve her former glory? Obadiah suggests that the future holds hope beyond the remnant. The glory of all Judah will be restored.

Not only will Judah be blessed with resurgence, but she will also have a destructive power equal to the Edomites' destructiveness.

Fire and *stubble* are images used to suggest God's judgment of evil (see Exodus 15:7; Isaiah 10:17; 29:5-6; Matthew 3:12; Luke 3:17).

His survivors evokes the memory of fleeing refugees captured by waiting Edomites (verse 14) and turned over to the Babylonians. Earlier oracles promised a remnant, that is, survivors, from the destruction. This oracle promises no survivors—no remnant whatsoever—from

Esau's (Edom's) coming destruction. The certainty of the promise is underscored by the expression *for the LORD has spoken.*

Intrinsic in the oracle is the latent danger of an arrogant nationalism within Judean thinking. Is Obadiah leading his people down the same path of ruin that Edom has walked? Is he leading his people to trust in their own might and power? Few things are worse than selfish nationalism wearing the cloak of divine authority.

Verse 18 concludes with the only possible corrective to the peril of nationalism. The victory of a restored Jerusalem is the Lord's victory. As the Lord once used foreign peoples as instruments against Edom, so the Lord will once again choose to use Judah.

Promise of Israel's Restoration (verses 19-21)

The land has always been a means by which God blesses or curses Israel. The land and its fertility are blessings. Loss of land or lack of fertility are curses. In this stanza in verses 19-20, Obadiah reaffirms the age-old promise of land as Israel's (recall God's promise to Abraham in Genesis 12:1-3).

Following the collapse of Judah and the sack of Jerusalem, Edomites began moving into the Negeb wilderness. Historically, the Negeb had been a part of Israelite and Judean territory. The name *Negeb* brackets this stanza, showing the extremities of territory that will once again be Judah's. What follows is a description of the counterattack that Judah will launch.

Shephelah (NRSV; NIV = foothills) means *lowlands*. It occupies the western foothills south of Israel. Its boundaries were the Valley of Aijalon to the north, a series of valleys to the east, Nahal Shiqma to the south, and the coastal plains to the west. The region was some twenty-eight miles long and nine miles wide. The most important town in the region was Lachish.

Gilead is in the territory east of the Jordan River, called the Transjordan.

Halah is a region in northern Mesopotamia (see 2 Kings 17:6) to which some exiles had been deported. These returnees will occupy the territory traditionally associated with the Phoenicians near the Mediterranean Sea.

Exiles from Jerusalem living in *Sepharad* (modern-day Turkey) will occupy the major cities of the Negeb.

Obadiah concludes his prophecy in verse 21, with two ringing affirmations. The first is a political-military image of warriors and others possessing the holy city, from which they will once again hold sway over their southern neighbor. But Obadiah goes further than military-political power. The final phrase calls to mind the greater hope that characterizes faith. Obadiah points to the coming of the Kingdom of God.

What service has Obadiah rendered? When confronted with an overwhelming political and military catastrophe, the people had to endure not only the immediate consequences. They also had to endure the bitterness of a collaborating kindred nation. An impulse of hatred stirred within each survivor.

For many, faith in God was swept away by the floods of disaster and despair. The tides of history had ripped their God from them. Obadiah courageously recovers for them a faith from history itself. Furthermore, this prophet's oracles condemn Edom's disregard for common origins, and they lift the people's vision to a higher and broader horizon. Eternal justice will prevail. Even though the judgment may be delayed, Obadiah still clings to the hope that the kingdom will finally be God's kingdom.

§ § § § § § §

The Message of Obadiah

Obadiah spoke to a defeated and demoralized nation. The arrogant strength of Edom had engulfed the people of God. Are arrogant nations more powerful than God? Obadiah's response is, No! What else can we learn from the prophet Obadiah?

§ When God acts, no defense is sufficient.
§ Even when God is silent, still God continues to work.
§ Pride goes before a fall.
§ Eventually and inevitably God will secure victory for the divine purposes in history.
§ In God's sight, it is criminal to rejoice over someone else's catastrophe.
§ No nation can long endure if it intends to limit God's love or limit its own moral obligations.

§ § § § § § §

Introduction to Jonah

The book of Jonah is unique. No other book contains such remarkable circumstances, miraculous rescues, human traits, peculiar reversals, or surprises. Because the book is unique, and because it contains what is one of the most quickly recognized stories in the Old Testament, it evokes more discussion and argument than many other books.

In contrast to other prophetic works that are collections of oracles, Jonah contains only one oracle (3:4). With one exception, Amos, all the other prophets pronounce their oracles in the hearing of their own people, in their home territory. Jonah must travel to the heart of the nation to which this oracle is proclaimed.

In Israel's tradition, many of those called to prophesy hesitated and argued with God about the task. Recall Moses arguing that he could not speak well (Exodus 3). Elijah, too, resisted God's summons to further work, citing his lack of support (1 Kings 19:4-18). Jeremiah argued that he was too young to do such work (Jeremiah 1). But in each of these instances, the prophet finally succumbed to the will of God.

In Jonah's story, the reluctant prophet does a good deal more than resist with an argument. Jonah actually denies his God's claim and attempts to flee from God's presence. Indeed, the entire first half of the story is of Jonah's refusal.

The name *Jonah* does occur in earlier tradition. Second Kings 14:25 lists the name as a prophet, the son of

Amittai of the region of Gath-hepher. A careful reading of the episode in Kings exhibits the prophet's concern for the expansion of national boundaries, with no further concern for God's will for the king, the social order, or the nation's behavior. He gives evidence of the same attitude of which the prophet Jonah is guilty.

The Nature of the Book

The story itself overflows with peculiar and spectacular phenomena. Had the writer been concerned primarily with an historically reliable series of events, the story would take on a different character. As it is, the story is replete with storytelling devices. The story is a parable.

Historical Circumstances

Determining the date of the book's composition is very difficult. Since the book is essentially a parable, it could easily have been composed at any time. Another book in the Old Testament, the book of Ruth, shares a similar ambiguity with regard to its date.

In Jonah, the major city Nineveh, to which the prophet is to travel, is referred to as a place in the remote past. The author cites two post-exilic prophets (Jeremiah and Joel), which gives evidence of a late date for the book's composition.

The Purpose of the Book

Jonah's outrage that his prophecy has been frustrated suggests that the purpose may center on the issue of unfulfilled prophecy. However, if 4:11 is the point toward which the entire book moves, then unfulfilled prophecy is too narrow a theme.

In the mind of the author and his audience, an all-powerful and sovereign God seemed terribly slow to punish the heathen for what they had done to God's chosen nation. Jonah's fear that the heathen might be spared represents a generally held apprehension. Through sensitive and human representation of these foreigners, Jonah forces his listeners to reconsider God's sovereignty. Against a popularly-held prejudice that relished the notion of God's punishment of enemies, Jonah lifts up the truth of God's compassion. God's care and compassion are equal to God's wrath and judgment.

In this work Jonah presents the possibility of repentance. The important question is not whether Nineveh could or would repent, but whether or not Israel could or would repent from a narrow, nationalistic view of God.

Introduction to These Chapters

The book of Jonah begins by introducing the story and setting the scene for the rest of the narrative.

Chapter 1 has two parts.
  I. The Great Refusal (1:1-3)
 II. Jonah Punished (1:4-16)

The Great Refusal (1:1-3)

The book begins with the word of the Lord coming to the prophet Jonah. In 1 Kings 17, Elijah's summons to prophesy is described with the same expression. Jeremiah's call to ministry is similar (Jeremiah 1:4). The identification of the source of the work establishes the authority of the work immediately.

However, the identification of Jonah's native territory would have surprised the listeners. Amittai lived in the Northern Kingdom. Strong nationalistic feelings ran deeply. This prophet of an earlier time had preached little more than nationalistic expansion (see 2 Kings 14:25). Therefore, the listeners would have a terrible tension. They would have to heed the divinely-authorized words of the prophet, while at the same time feeling deep resentment against the national origin of the prophet.

God's instructions to Jonah are similar to those given to Elijah, *Go now* (see 1 Kings 17:8-9).

Nineveh was, until its collapse in 612 B.C., the capital city of the Assyrian empire. The city was located on the left bank of the Tigris River. The great city had been characterized by earlier writers as arrogant (see 2 Kings 18:28; Isaiah 10:12-14), and particularly cruel (see Nahum 3:19).

Unlike other prophets who proclaimed their words within the safe confines of their native territory, Jonah is required to go to the center of the offending national capital. He will not enjoy the relative calm of preaching to the already converted.

While resistance to the divine summons is not without precedent (Moses in Exodus 4:10, 13; Jeremiah in 1:6), the actual fleeing away from the presence of God is. Why did the prophet attempt to flee? The narrator gives no indication. Perhaps Jonah already sensed that God's intentions differed from his own desire that the evil city be punished (see 4:2). Jonah may simply have been apprehensive. It is one thing to preach to a specific individual such as a king or a priest. It is yet another thing to preach to an entire city of strangers. All of this is conjecture on our part, and clearly not a concern for the narrator.

Tarshish is generally thought of as a part of Spain (see Isaiah 23:1-12; Ezekiel 27:12). The impression given is that Jonah attempted to flee as far away as possible from God and the designated city.

Jonah Punished (1:4-16)

Jonah's attempted flight from the Lord is a futile one. The Lord accompanies the reluctant prophet even on the sea. Indeed, the Lord works through the tempest of an ocean storm. Jonah cannot escape the presence of God. (See also Psalms 65:5-7; 107:23-32; 139:7-12; Jeremiah 23:19-20.)

With a minimum of words the narrator describes the panic on board the vessel. Sailors pray desperate prayers to their individual gods. Note how cleverly the narrator asserts the futility of smaller religions against the reality of God's sovereign power. Equipment is tossed overboard. But even these desperate efforts are not sufficient. The sailors have been caught up in the consequences of another's sin.

The captain of the vessel approaches the sleeping prophet with an insight the prophet himself is slow to learn. The storm is not an ordinary storm. This storm is caused by Jonah's God. The captain suggests the possibility of God's saving protection. The narrator thus portrays the heathen captain as more perceptive and open to the graces of God than the prophet himself.

Casting lots to determine outcome is mentioned in other places. In 1 Samuel 14:40-42, lots are cast to determine guilt.

The terrified crew demands a confession from Jonah. Now the prophet has to state his sin in his own words. Note that nation and religion/God go together. In ancient times, God and nation were inextricably joined. *Hebrew* is how the people identified themselves (see Exodus 3:18).

While Jonah is able to affirm God's sovereignty over land and sea (hence his calm during the tempest), he is unable to comprehend or accept God's sovereign will that must be obeyed by both nation and individual.

In verses 10-12, the sailors demand an explanation, since they see in Jonah both explanation for and the means by which to calm the storm. Evidently Jonah's conscience has been stirred. The sailors are desperate. Their plight is largely the result of Jonah's sin. His willingness to die indicates his tacit acknowledgment of his guilt.

Even after Jonah's confession, the sailors attempt to save themselves. Nothing less than the death of the sinner will suffice (see Ezekiel 18:4, 20).

The sailors do what the reluctant prophet did not do.

They pray that they may not be guilty of taking life. Jonah's inevitable punishment arrives. He is tossed into the raging sea, whereupon the storm ceases almost immediately. The ironic twist is that the reluctant prophet who did not want to become a missionary to the heathen ends up doing a missionary work. The result of Jonah's sacrifice is that the sailors now believe.

The story's structure illustrates the author's genius. The real hero of the story is not Jonah, nor is it the heathen sailors. The real hero is God, who can use both human beings and natural forces to bring about belief. God can use many different means through which to reveal God's power.

§ § § § § § §

The Message of Jonah 1

The remarkable parable of the reluctant prophet reveals God, who intends to accomplish a dual purpose. First, the prophet will learn that he must obey the command of God. Second, the audience will learn through Jonah's experience that God's intention transcends their limited vision of God's sovereignty. The story begins with the word of God. God's word and work are always a moral work. Even a person who attempts to avoid God can be used by God to achieve God's purposes. What can we learn about ourselves and God through this chapter?

§ The command of God may threaten our preconceptions and our wishes.

§ The path of self-will is always away from God and toward our own destruction.

§ Any attempt to flee from either the call of God or the presence of God is futile.

§ God will use any means necessary to reveal the divine purposes.

§ In every human spirit there is a yearning to know God.

§ Sometimes it takes a storm in order to stir the deepest yearnings for God.

§ Confession of our identity and our highest calling reveals our basic sinfulness.

§ God does not turn from us when we turn from God.

§ People do not necessarily have to know God in order to have God know and care for them.

§ § § § § § §

Jonah 2–4

Introduction to These Chapters

In our English Bibles, the narrative of Jonah's plight continues with verse 17. In the Hebrew Old Testament, the narrative divides at the beginning of chapter 2. Since the story takes on a new emphasis, the Hebrew division will be followed at this point.

Whenever Israel looked out to the west and saw the Mediterranean Sea, images of monsters were conjured up. The Hebrews were never a seagoing people. The sea therefore represented a great life-threatening force. The writer could hardly have shown Jonah in a worse plight than cast overboard in the midst of a raging storm. Perhaps the more imaginative listeners could discern in the story Israel's own story.

Assuming the book is a relatively late composition, then the entire listening audience could easily draw on the historical memory of the horror of national collapse, widespread despair, deportation into a foreign land, and languishing in exile. Fully two generations would pass before the Hebrews were allowed to return to their beloved land. Once the years began dragging into generations, few could imagine the return. Fewer still could imagine how the return would be accomplished. A non-Jew, the Persian King Cyrus, issued an edict giving release to the captives.

As the story of Jonah continues in the following verses, the author expresses through a psalm the experience of Israel's national death and resurrection.

Jonah 2–4 may be outlined as follows.

I. Jonah Rescued (1:17–2:10)
II. The Great Mission (3:1–4:11)
   A. Jonah's obedience (3:1-4)
   B. Nineveh's repentance (3:5-9)
   C. Jonah's rebuke (3:10–4:11)

Jonah Rescued (1:17–2:10)

Jonah's plight is quite hopeless. Without some sort of intervention, he is a doomed man. In the midst of the chaos, God appoints a great fish to swallow Jonah in an act of protection.

Any attempt to justify the story with biological explanations will lead inevitably to frustration. The more significant question has to do with the meaning of the fish in the story. The great fish stands for the unmerited grace of God who, though offended by a reluctant and fleeing prophet, refuses to allow the man's death. Through no merit of his own, Jonah is saved from certain death.

The three days and nights should not be interpreted as a reference to the time Jesus spent in the tomb. Rather, the time emphasizes the length of an important journey (see Genesis 22, where Abraham and Isaac travel some three days' journey to the mountain). The Hebrew language has a minimum of adjectives. Any emphasis must be achieved through repetition of verbs. Therefore, instead of saying "Jonah stayed for a very long time," the narrator uses the period of three days for emphasis.

We might expect Jonah to launch into an immediate plea for help and rescue. However, the narrative continues in verse 1 of chapter 3 with Jonah proclaiming a psalm of thanksgiving.

The psalm consists of three stanzas (verses 2-4, 5-7, and 8-9). Using a well-known liturgical formula, the author shows Jonah telling of a personal crisis from which he has been rescued by divine intervention.

In the first stanza (verses 2-4), Jonah acknowledges the fact that he has been rescued from certain death. *Sheol* (also called the *Pit* in verse 6) is the land of darkness and death (see also Psalm 88:3-12; Proverbs 1:12; Isaiah 5:14).

At death's door, Jonah's concern is that he will not be able to worship; Jonah discloses his anxiety that he has been cut off from the presence of God. Note how the litany parallels the national catastrophe of defeat and exile. Exiles too wondered how they could worship. *How could we sing the LORD's song in a foreign land?* (Psalm 137:4).

The second stanza of Jonah's psalm (verses 5-7) alludes to God's action in the past. Here details are given of the event in verse 3. The images are of a man within a moment of death with absolutely no hope. Incredibly, God intervenes and lifts the drowning man from his desperate plight. In Jonah's instance, of course, the images are of drowning. But the images can also be interpreted as metaphors to describe other circumstances that felt as if they had threatened life itself.

The *Sheol* means *the grave* (see Psalm 88:3-12).

The prophet has a special relationship with God. However, prayer that is available for all persons is shown as the central element of Jonah's own responsibility.

The final stanza of the psalm (verses 8-9) alludes to the futile practice of idolatry. True religion and true faith take their cue from the reality of God, who is approachable through prayer. God had heeded the prayers of the heathen sailors earlier. Now God has heard the prayers of a reluctant prophet. Could the author be suggesting that the prayer itself is the important aspect, rather than the character of the individual offering the prayer? If so, then the argument is even stronger against individual or national pride and exclusivity.

Recognition of God's grace and protection evokes within the prophet the desire to worship in the Temple.

Jonah's spirit has been humbled by God's grace. His attempt to flee from the responsibility of mission took him within a hair's breadth of death. Only the grace of God protected him. Now Jonah considers God's saving action the utterly gracious gift that it has always been. God would not allow Jonah to flee. Jonah has now come full circle. He wants to be in the presence of God.

The fish, having served its purpose, deposits the reluctant prophet onto the beach.

Jonah's Obedience (3:1-4)

The second half of the book begins with Jonah's second summons to prophetic ministry. The grace of God is again illustrated, since Jonah did not suffer the fate that another prophet suffered. In 1 Kings 13, a story is told of a prophet who disobeys God's command. When that prophet eats and drinks against God's order, he is killed by a lion. Recognizing how fortunate and protected he has been, Jonah now listens to a command he had previously rejected.

Since the great city needs description, scholars have concluded that the book itself is a later work. Nineveh exists only in the memory by the time Jonah is written. The city has a circumference of seven and one-half miles. The sheer size of the city gives evidence of the overwhelming task set before Jonah.

The forty-day period is a grace period. The tradition of forty is common: the Israelites wandered for forty years in the wilderness; in Deuteronomy 9:18-25 Moses offers forty days of supplication. In the New Testament, Jesus' temptation lasts for forty days.

Nineveh's Repentance (3:5-9)

The city repents. The multitudes act as immediately in the face of their crisis as did the desperate sailors when they faced imminent death (see 1:5).

The people's repentance is authentic. They not only

believe, they act out their belief through common rituals. A fast is proclaimed (see Jeremiah 36:9). They put on sackcloth, the attire symbolic of repentance (see 2 Samuel 3:31; 1 Kings 21:27; Daniel 9:3).

Even the king adheres to the acts and reinforces them through personal behavior and proclamation of an official edict (see verses 6-8).

The author has shown a long-detested enemy hearing the word of God through the prophet, and immediately repenting, from the highest to the lowest station in life.

Even the animals of the territory are included in the act. Recall that in Joel the animals pray during the awful drought (see Joel 1:20).

The author cleverly shows the pagans understanding that repentance needs to be something in addition to ritual and rite. Could the author be suggesting in a subtle way that Israel itself has overlooked this critical notion? True repentance has a moral character to it. The king demands a change in his people.

The violence refers to violations of basic human rights (see Amos 3:10; Micah 6:12).

From the mouth of a pagan (verse 9) comes the recognition that even the most authentic repentance does not obligate God. From a pagan comes the insight that God is still a sovereign God, utterly free to choose subsequent action. Joel's insight in 2:14, Amos's suggestion in 9:7, and the pagan's words stun the listeners with their remarkable insight into the nature and character of Israel and God. Israel wanted to believe that appropriate religious behavior in some sense obligated God to act benevolently towards the nation. Prophet and pagan alike acknowledge God's freedom.

Jonah's Rebuke (3:10–4:11)

When God sees the authentic repentance (verse 10), God repents from the planned destruction (recall Amos's intercessions and God's changed mind in Amos 7:1-6).

The listener might now expect Jonah, the one who was once himself in a desperate situation and then rescued, to rejoice, since the great multitudes of Nineveh will not die.

Through one individual, the author exposes the attitude of the nation. Like Jonah, the nation has continued to cherish her hatred of the enemy. Though they might have earned a certain kinship through their own suffering and deliverance, they chose instead to relish animosity and anticipate destruction and death.

When God ceases being angry with Nineveh, Jonah becomes extremely angry. Jonah's anger does two things. First, it blinds him to his own experience of salvation and grace. Second, it causes Jonah to condemn himself with every word.

Jonah's response is similar to Elijah's response in 1 Kings 19:1-18. There Elijah had successfully proven that God is the Lord during the trial by fire on Mount Carmel. But he fled into the wilderness and there wished only to die (see 1 Kings 19:4). However, in the Elijah narrative, Elijah is jealous *for* God. In Jonah's narrative, Jonah is jealous *of* God.

Jonah's attempted flight to Tarshish had been triggered by the character of God. God's love is for all people. This insight causes Jonah grief and consternation. Better that he should die than to have to live with the reality of this truth. As Jonah could not accept this truth, neither could Israel. When confronted and challenged by a larger God than he has imagined, Jonah wishes to cease living. Jonah's God is too small. And Jonah's God will not allow Jonah to harbor a small God in the midst of a grand creation.

God's question in verse 4 is a rhetorical one, intending to evoke a negative response.

The city is mentioned three times in a single verse (verse 5). Thus the author focuses attention on the city in sharp contrast to Jonah's own stubborn behavior and attitude. Jonah has built a temporary shelter from which he will be able to view the destruction of the city. Evidently the shelter is not enough to keep the oppressive sun from him. Now God, who had earlier supplied a saving fish, supplies a saving plant to shade the prophet.

The name for God changes in verse 6. Here the name LORD God is used.

The bush is a castor oil plant or a ricinus plant.

In verses 7-8 Jonah is still blinded by his hatred and jealousy. Even though he himself has been the recipient of many graces, he still wants the city destroyed. Not yet ready to disclose the entire meaning, God sends a worm, perhaps a weevil, to destroy the plant. When the scorching sirocco comes, Jonah will be defenseless.

Previously Jonah had ignored God's question (see verse 4). Now Jonah is sufficiently distressed as to cast all caution to the wind. Readers can better imagine the answer if they can hear his response as something very much like cursing.

The final scene of the entire parable unfolds in verse 10. God's analysis of Jonah's anger reveals its selfishness. Jonah had been primarily concerned about his own protection from the noonday sun. Jonah gave not a first thought to the unfortunate people in the city. Against the reluctant prophet's small-minded attitude, God places the compassion for vast numbers of people.

The city is populated by people who do not know their right hand from their left—they are spiritually ignorant and immature people. They need help and compassion, not condemnation and punishment.

The book clearly illustrates God's concern for all creatures great and small. God is vitally concerned and involved with all the creation, not merely the chosen or those who believe themselves to be God's elect.

§ § § § § § §

The Message of Jonah 2–4

Through a parable the author has brought a new insight to a reluctant people. God's concern and compassion are for all the creation. What else can we learn from this story?

§ We can limit God's love and will through our own disobedience.

§ When God calls an individual to a specific task, that task cannot be taken lightly.

§ The protection and grace we receive in life are gifts and graces from God.

§ God respects true repentance, no matter who it comes from.

§ God does not want to be known as a small God with limited perspectives and limited concern for persons.

§ God wants us to love all creation as God loves all creation.

§ We learn of God's revelation through our own experiences and through the character of God.

§ Sometimes God's love haunts us as much as it blesses us.

§ In the face of life's storms, both believer and pagan are equally in need of God's mercy.

§ § § § § § §

Glossary of Terms

Ahaz: The name means *he has grasped*. King of Judah from 735-715 B.C. The son and successor of Jotham. Remembered for his evil practices.

Amaziah: The name means *Yahu is strong*. King of Judah in 800-783 B.C. Only twenty-five when he began to reign, he immediately killed those who had assassinated his father (2 Kings 14:5-6). Reconquered Edomite territory and was later assassinated.

Amittai: The name means *true*. Father of the prophet Jonah.

Ammon: Descendant of Lot (see Genesis 19:38). Originally occupied the area of southern Transjordan, later called Moab. Conquered by David and later by Solomon.

Ashdod: One of the five principal Philistine cities. It was located halfway between Gaza and Joppa.

Ashkelon: One of the five main Philistine cities, located on the Mediterranean seacoast. It was twelve miles north of Gaza and ten miles south of Ashdod.

Assyrians: The first of the major empires of the Mesopotamian region. The name stems from the name of the major city, Asshur. Famous rulers were Tiglath-pileser III and Shalmaneser. Later the empire was replaced by the Babylonian empire.

Aven, Valley of: The name means *wickedness*. Hosea refers to high places of Aven (10:8). Aven is used in combination with other names to indicate evil.

Baal: The name means *master*, or occasionally *husband*. Throughout her history, Israel had to contend with the inclination among her people to assimilate Canaanite religious rites related to Baal.

Babylonia: Replaced the once-powerful Assyrian empire. Judah and Jerusalem were conquered by the Babylonians in 587 B.C.

Bashan: The northern portion of the area east of the Jordan River. Tableland with fruitful and stoneless plains where livestock was raised.

Ben-Hadad: King of Damascus who followed his father Hazael to the throne in 798 B.C. (2 Kings 13).

Beth-aven: A combination of words meaning *house of wickedness* and *evil*. Hosea uses the term as a derogatory reference to the city of Bethel.

Bethel: A city in the territory of Benjamin. For the Canaanites it was a sanctuary city dedicated to their god, El. Amos prophesied here.

Bozrah: An Edomite fortress city, symbolizing Edom's strength. The name means *fortified place.*

Carmel: A mountain on the coast of Palestine. It plays an important role in the work of Elijah and Elisha.

Damascus: The capital city of the Syrian kingdom.

Edom: The region adjacent to Israel to the east and south.

Ekron: The northernmost of the five principal cities of the Philistines.

Ephod: A priestly garment.

Esau: One of the sons of Isaac and Rebekah; the elder twin brother of Jacob. Ancestor of the Edomites.

Gaza: A Philistine city in southwest Palestine.

Gibeon: A city of the tribe of Benjamin, six miles southwest of Jerusalem.

Gomer: The wife of the prophet Hosea. Her unfaithfulness in marriage is used as an example of Israel's unfaithfulness to God.

Hazael: He seized the Syrian throne in 831 B.C.

Hezekiah: King of Judah from 715-687 B.C.; the son and

successor of Ahaz.

Homer: A unit of dry measure that equals about 5.16 bushels.

Jeroboam: Chosen as the first king of Israel, in 922 B.C.

Jezreel: A fertile valley separating Samaria from Galilee.

Jotham: The son of Uzziah, the twelfth king of Judah.

Kerioth: The fortified capital city of Moab.

Lebanon: A mountain range in Syria.

Lethech: A unit of dry measure that equals about 2.5 bushels.

Moab: A state in the Transjordan, east of the Dead Sea.

Negeb: A desert region in southern Palestine.

Nineveh: The capital city of the Assyrian empire; the appointed destination of the prophet Jonah.

Philistines: Sea people who occupied the southern coast of Palestine.

Samaria: The capital city of the Northern Kingdom, Israel. Also refers to the hill country of Palestine.

Shekel: Originally meant a unit of weight; later referred to a coin weighing half an ounce.

Sheol: The abode of the dead.

Shephelah: A lowland area between the Judean highlands and the coastal plains of Philistia.

Tekoa: A city close to Bethlehem; the home of Amos.

Teraphim: Small and portable idols.

Tarshish: The place to which Jonah attempted to flee; its location is uncertain.

Uzziah: The king of Judah from 783 to 742 B.C.; son and successor of Amaziah.

Guide to Pronunciation

Ahaz: AY-haz
Achor: Ah-CORE
Admah: AHD-mah
Amaziah: Aa-mah-ZIGH-ah
Assyria: Ah-SEER-ee-ah
Aven: Ah-VEN
Baal: Bah-AHL
Baalam: BAY-lam
Baal-peor: Bah-AHL-peh-ORE
Beth-eden: Beth-ay-DEN
Diblaim: Dib-LIGH-im
Edom: EE-dom
Ephraim: Ee-frah-EEM
Gibeah: GIH-bee-ah
Gilead: GIH-lee-ad
Gilgal: GIL-gal
Halah: Hah-LAH
Hezekiah: Heh-zeh-KIGH-ah
Jezreel: Jez-REEL
Jeroboam: Jer-oh-BOH-am
Joash: JOH-ash
Joppa: JAH-puh
Jotham: JOH-tham
Mizpah: MIZ-pah
Moresheth: MORE-eh-sheth
Negeb: NEH-geb

Nineveh: NIH-neh-veh
Pethuel: Peh-THOO-ell
Philistines: FILL-iss-teens
Rabbah: Rah-BAH
Ramah: Rah-MAH
Shephelah: Sheh-FAY-lah
Tabor: Tay-BORE
Tekoa: Teh-KOH-ah
Teman: Tay-MAHN
Uzziah: Oo-ZIGH-ah
Zeboiim: Zeh-BOH-eem